Praise for

THE COURAGE TO BECOME

"*The Courage to Become* beautifully and honestly shares a story that so many women live every day. We are always becoming—something new, something feared, something previously unknown. When I became a spouse, and then a mother, I went through the looking glass—seeing myself as I had been, not recognizing who I was to become, but mostly feeling lost and alone in the desert that bridged the two.

I know now that I was not alone in my struggle to become. Catia's story is remarkable in its candor and relatability. The humor, compassion and earnestness in her storytelling, combined with the readability of a friend's journal make *The Courage to Become* a gift I would give to any new mother, spouse, or friend looking for a companion on the journey."

—STEPHANIE OWENS
    feminist, sister, auntie, mama, and avid reader

"*Finally* a book that details all the things *you wish you knew* about pregnancy and early motherhood. *The Courage to Become* provides *reassurance* for the moment and *hope* for the future as you journey through these exciting and often challenging seasons. As a mother of two and a practicing Ob/Gyn for 15 years, I know this book is a valuable guiding light."

—DONELL OLIVER
    MD, Obstetrics and Gynecology

"A heartfelt guide to honest living, told with vulnerability, courage, and humor. *The Courage to Become* harnesses life's bittersweet contradictions—from the perseverance to fight through life's challenges, to surrendering to life's wild ride. It's the perfect companion for a young woman tackling life with a full heart."

—ARIANA MCLAUGHLIN
    journalist, sister, daughter, and 'Tia Anna'

The

Courage

to

Become

Feel the Fear and do act Anyway

The
Courage
to
Become

Stories of Hope for Navigating
Love, Marriage and Motherhood

CATIA HERNANDEZ HOLM

Cover design by Sheila Parr
Cover image © Lev Kropotov / Shutterstock

ISBN: 978-0-9983782-0-6

Printed in the United States of America

To my husband and daughters,
loving you has been the pleasure of my life.

"When you get, give; when you learn, teach."

—Maya Angelou

CONTENTS

FOREWORD

In *The Courage to Become*, Catia puts it all out there. She gives us a front-row seat to so many private, uncomfortable moments during her journey through love, marriage, and motherhood, all in the name of solidarity. She wants us to know what she went through, not only to share her story, but more importantly, to let us know that we are not alone.

I feel awfully lucky that I've *become* a lot of amazing things. I've become a wife, a mother, and a friend to countless wonderful people, but I've also had the blessing of becoming the owner of a business that empowers women, *Austin Moms Blog*, and most recently, *Waco Moms Blog*. Each are locally focused parenting websites written by local moms, for local moms. And even though our reach is now over eight million, it wasn't always that way.

Our team of sixty writers share their experiences with motherhood, which run the gamut from hysterical to heartbreaking. Catia has been a part of our team for years. Now, six years later, *Austin Moms Blog* and *Waco Moms Blog* are powerful forces.

I remember asking Catia why she wanted to join us; we were only twenty-five women back then. She said it was because *Austin Moms Blog* had given her hope during middle-of-the-night feeding sessions, and she wanted to give back.

That's what I love about *The Courage to Become*. It's part comfort, but it's also part hope and encouragement.

Moments when I felt isolated during my motherhood journey included when my firstborn missed every major developmental milestone. It often sent me into a state of panic. Had I known I wasn't alone, maybe I wouldn't have dwelled on it so much.

And while my husband and I were dating, I wish someone would have pulled me aside and encouraged me to relish and enjoy that new season of life. We had so much free time then!

Whether these challenges have to do with parenting or motherhood, knowing that it's not just me is extremely comforting and relieving. I'm blessed to be surrounded by amazing cheerleaders and friends. *The Courage to Become* armors us with tools to live with purpose and joy and, above all, encourages us to believe that not only are we enough, we are plenty, just as we are.

As Catia's friend and sister in motherhood, I can tell you that positivity pours out of her and that she has an inner light that beams from her soul. She smiles from ear to ear, which connects her with everyone she encounters. She genuinely makes an effort to appreciate people for who they really are. Whether she's writing, loving her family, or creating community, Catia approaches everything with excellence, passion, and gratitude.

May you find comfort and encouragement within these pages.

—ALLISON MACK, daughter, sister, wife, mother of three
Co-founder of *Austin Moms Blog* and *Waco Moms Blog*
Austin, Texas

INTRODUCTION

Have you ever been out on a trail and noticed neon-colored pin flags? The pin flags were put there by someone who traveled that route before you. They are there to mark the trail, to signal the twists and turns and even the gentle curves of the path ahead. When seen all together, the pin flags communicate a suggested route. And even though each traveler is welcome to follow the pin flags, they are also welcome to deviate from the path. The flags are just a proposed path. The flags say someone has been here before; you are safe, and it is okay.

Each chapter in this book is a pin flag, a point where the trail of my life turned.

In 2012, I identified as a career woman. In 2015, I identified as a wife and mother. During that three-year span, the rhythm of my life was steady and strong; changes presented themselves one right after the other. And with each change came the opportunity to adjust or get steamrolled. This book recounts those milestones of growth I experienced from 2012 to 2015, from dating to marriage and into the beginning stages of motherhood.

During those years, I gleaned advice and information from all sorts of books and people, and yet there was an information void. I wanted a blueprint; I wanted to see pin flags. I wanted to know other women had traveled the same path. I wanted a woman to show me how she navigated being a new wife and a new mama. I wanted a real account of a real woman. I wanted to see myself in her, know that she had traveled this route before me, so I could believe I was going to be okay. But I could never quite find that account, so I wrote it. I wrote a book flagging the contours of these life seasons.

I'm sharing my story with the hope that women will find peace in knowing they are not alone, that a sisterhood of women has also traveled this path, and that not only can they survive this season, but they can thrive.

For various reasons, most of the names of the sweet souls that have helped me along the way have been changed, except for my ever-loving family. And it must be noted that my interpretations of teachings from gurus, theologians, authors, pastors, and doctors are purely personal; I am not anyone's spokesperson.

You will also note that each chapter contains a *Hope for Navigating* section, a place where I candidly express defeats as well triumphs, and the life lessons I learned from each, with the hope of giving you the confidence you need to continue your trajectory or change direction as needed. Life is a journey, and we can all benefit from those who have gone before us, alerting us to what may come next, be it a bump in the road or a scenic overlook. Finally, at the end of each chapter, there are trail journal questions, just for you. These questions are not meant to be answered all at once. They are meant to plant seeds and start conversations about where your life is now and where you would like it to go next.

Chapter 1

MEETING "THE ONE"

yup.

He was honest, steady, and radiated peace. He was a man, fully realized. An image of a unicorn came to mind unbidden. I had read about fully realized men, but I had never seen one in person.

The evening of our first date, I gave him directions. "Drive up to the gate, take a left at the first stop sign, and take a right at the next building." It had been years since a man had gone out of his way to pick me up for dinner.

As he drove up to my building, I nonchalantly walked outside and waved him in the direction of my front door. I floated out, "Oh, hi. I'm not quite ready yet. I need a few more minutes." I appeared casual, but the reality was that I had strategized ALL day about what I would wear. I wanted to catch his eye but not be too done up. I fretted about everything, from my dress choice to my shoe choice. I wanted the dress to be pretty but not too loud, form-fitting but not *too* form-fitting, and showing off a little skin but not *too* much skin. When I walked out to greet him, I knew he would think I looked nice, but I also knew he was the kind of man who was looking for a lot more than that.

We went to a small café, painted peach with an airy island feel. I was on a real date, the kind of date my mother would approve of! The server seated us at small table out of the flow of traffic, so I knew I would not be able to feign distraction. We would actually have a conversation.

We ran out of niceties after our first course, and my personal blog became a topic of conversation. In my revealing blog, I detailed my life's defeats and triumphs, both large and small, but my frankness did not serve me well in the dating department. Would he or would he not end up as part of Wednesday's entry? *Stay tuned.*

The server cleared our autumn squash soups, and our conversation turned to my dating choices. He had read a few of my posts, which both flattered and embarrassed me. I mean, he had material with which to analyze me, and I didn't even know where he had gone to college.

"I don't think you're ready to date a nice guy. I'll date you, but I don't think you're ready." OMG! !!

BOMB.

"EXCUSE me?"

What in the world? Explosions went off in my head, my ego convulsed, my head spun. I did not know what to do. *Unicorns attack?* LOL

I needed time to think, so I excused myself and went to the ladies' room. I had gone through an entire day's worth of preparation to be irritated? Insulted? My buttons had been more than pushed. Was there some truth to his statement? Heart racing, I walked into the restroom, closed the door behind me, and took a few deep breaths. I reapplied my wild berry lip stain and adjusted the black dress that had taken me hours to decide upon. Gripping the sides of the cold ceramic sink, I took a long look at myself in the mirror.

You can do this. Who does this guy think he is? He hardly knows you. You ARE ready for a nice guy. You deserve a nice guy. Hell, a nice guy deserves YOU!

I didn't know if my date thought of himself as a nice guy, or even if *I* thought he was a nice guy. What I *did* know was that his comment had struck a nerve. Yes, some of my past behavior had proven his point, but I had since evolved—so there was a chance he was wrong. I couldn't put my finger on it, but my intuition told me that this situation was different. So, waltzing the twenty yards back to the table, I checked myself before I wrecked myself. I made a conscious decision to not be steered by my initial reaction.

Makeup freshened, I sat down.

"I'll take you home if you'd like."

I guess he could sense I was put off. "I'm fine, thanks." My decade-long career in customer service had helped me craft a charming conversational shtick; I had a reservoir of quips, sports trivia, and banter that never failed me. But since I had an inkling that Anthony was different, I threw that standard shtick out the window and, for better or worse, *committed to being authentic.* According to Danielle LaPorte, "the universe cannot resist authenticity." *Amen to this.*

I had always tried my best to be what the guy sitting across from me wanted. "Like to hunt? Me too! Like to fish? Me too! Like to watch sports all day? So do I!" Obviously, that strategy had not served me well. This time around, I wouldn't do any of that. I wanted to show up and be real. This time I was going to be genuine, and I was going to prove to myself that I was ready for a nice guy. Come hell or high water, I was going to honor kindness in a man.

Just Between Us

I had a list of failed relationships. I was quick to force situations so much so that these relationships exploded; I was unwilling to just let things unfold. I had terrible self-esteem, and I constantly hustled for the approval of men. I lived in the swamps of romance, constantly muddied.

Even though we've been told that failure is about perspective and is really an opportunity for learning, consistent failure is dejecting. Every perceived failure chips away at our confidence and eventually our self-worth. If you have navigated the dating scene for a long time without the ultimate reward of an all-encompassing love, you start to wonder if you will be relegated to a life alone.

I'm sure you've navigated your own muddy waters in the swamps of romance, and you may have even kissed a few princes who turned out to be frogs. You may wonder if there is anyone out there who could possibly love all of you and be worthy of your devotion in return. But, according to Elizabeth Gilbert in *Eat Pray Love*, "ruin is a gift; ruin is the road to transformation."

In 2012, in a search for guidance and in hopes of finding unconditional love, I settled into a good church home. As a result, my relationship with God deepened. One Sunday, our pastor preached, "Maybe God is directing your path away from big blessings because he knows you're not ready to handle the size of the blessing on its way. Maybe you are in a space where you would be unable to honor the blessing. Maybe God is waiting until you're ready."

Light bulb. Huge light bulb!

After I heard that, I devoted myself to showing God that I could and would honor people and that I was trustworthy. I wanted him to know I would be a good steward of his blessings.

It only took a few dates with Anthony for me to realize that the man I was spending time with was a nice guy, and that he was *the* nice guy I wanted to honor. My intuition called out, "Pay close attention here. Proceed wisely." Moment by moment, choice by choice, I honored Anthony, and that conscious awareness, that sacred abiding, catapulted me into greater blessings.

Hope for Navigating—Finding "The One"

The term "the one" can be charged with angst. Culture tells us we need "the one," but I beg to differ. We need to be "the one" for ourselves before we can be "the one" for someone else.

We need to be "the one" for ourselves before we can be "the one" for someone else.

When we are searching for "the one," we are in a perfect spot because we have the opportunity to draw the type of person we want. The universal laws of attraction are miraculous in that way. Our greatest asset is not only declaring who we are, but living it. What kind of person do you want to be? What does a great day look like? What does a fulfilling relationship look like? Let's get clear on who we are and what we want, and then live it out.

Throughout this leg of our journeys, let's pay close attention and listen to our intuition. Then we'll have a better chance of making good decisions—decisions that, over time, create character and eventually a life. When you begin to embody your beliefs and conduct yourself in a way that brings you joy, the world will send you just who you've been looking for.

"We accept the love we think we deserve."
—Stephen Chbosky

Trail Journal

What steps do you want to take to be a good partner for somebody?

Love myself.

What qualities are you looking for in "the one"?

authentic + true. Trustworthy. honest.

What kind of love do you think you deserve?

If i'm honest, not too much.

Chapter 2

TAKING A LEAP

When Anthony and I met, I was a busy woman. I worked for my parents' company in the Rio Grande Valley, *and* I worked as the general manager of bar operations at a music theatre in downtown Austin. It was the perfect situation. Both jobs were fun, flexible, and allowed me freedom. Working for my parents, I filmed television segments, participated in community events, and developed our company culture. The general manager position was a sweet gig too! My boss was also my friend and mentor, and our relationship dated back ten years. He had been guiding me since before I could legally have a beer. We set goals, broke sales records, and belly laughed together every single day. We were so close that I used to tell him I'd donate my kidney if he ever needed one. I worked alongside an amazing team of bartenders, ushers, and operations folks, *and* I saw thousands of musicians play to adoring fans. While I worked, Jay Z performed "New York State of Mind," Tim McGraw brought down the house, and I danced and forged friendships. It was a dream!

And beyond the incredible experiences, I earned a hefty income. I loved it! I didn't have to ask anyone for a damn thing. I paid for meals for my friends, bought all the shoes I wanted, and picked up rounds and rounds of salted margaritas. I worked long hours and was rewarded for it. It was fantastic!

But with all the positives, there was one glaring problem: I worked so many hours that I could only spend slivers of time with Anthony. While Anthony enjoyed time with his friends or celebrated holidays, I worked. As a single person, working hours that ranged from nine in the morning to three the next morning had been great, but working *and* accommodating Anthony's schedule proved difficult. After a few months of unsuccessfully juggling my career and our relationship, I knew something had to give.

I heard Dr. Laura Berman once say that if you want a romantic relationship, you should make room for it in your life. If there's no landing space for a potential mate, that potential mate will just see themselves into another situation—one where they feel wanted and welcomed. And since I was particularly busy and self-sufficient, this notion stuck with me.

I loved Anthony, and I wanted a future with him. I wanted to make space for him before he saw himself out of the relationship. *But how?* The biggest impediment to furthering our relationship was lack of time—time to gather shared experiences, time to be spontaneous. So in an effort to remedy that, I decided to leave my gem of a job at the music theatre. But how in the world would I present this to Anthony? I'd have to weave it into casual conversation.

I was standing on the patio at the music theatre one afternoon. Dusk was on the horizon, and the concert doors were about to open to the public. I called Anthony to see how his day had gone, pacing the entire concrete patio. We exchanged small talk, and when the time felt just right, I leapt. "So, I was thinking, if you're going to be traveling a lot, I'd like to be home more … when you're home. I know I work most weekends and late hours and … I want to see you more." I was fumbling. "What do you think about that?" I asked in a high-pitched voice. "What do you think about me leaving my job here?"

Did I just mess up monumentally? Shit. I nervously awaited his answer. But without missing a beat, he said he supported my decision, and we agreed to set up a timeline. *Whew!*

About a month later, Anthony called for our afternoon chat. He told me about his workday, and I dropped in, mid-conversation, that I had just given a 45-day notice at work. Clearing his throat, he replied, "You put in your notice? Uh … good. Are you okay?" His tone of voice changed, and I felt the energy shift. I could only guess what he was thinking: *Holy shit, she wasn't joking. She is serious about wanting a life with me.*

So on June 16, 2013, with much sadness but also a booming hope for my future, I worked my last shift at the music theatre. I was sad, but I knew it was time to go. I had traded money and independence for the possibility of a deeper, more fulfilling relationship with the man I loved so much.

Just Between Us

Giving up my job was more than a financial change; it was a symbol of my commitment, a leap of faith. It was me saying, "I'm serious about wanting this to work, and I trust you." I knew Anthony and I would do fine with the loss of my wages, but I wasn't sure our nearly year-long relationship would be able to absorb the loss of an entirely independent woman. After all, I had worked hard to be me!

I had a complicated relationship with money. I believed money equaled power. I was wrong. GIRL, Same.

Money does not equal power.
Power is steadfast.
Power is truth.
Power is quiet.
Power is gentle.
Money is just money.

I hadn't reconciled that yet, and since I was making less money, I felt less powerful and scared. What if it didn't work? I had given up a portion of my career!

Not only did I feel less powerful and more dependent, but I also felt I had to make up for lost wages by working harder on the home front. I went from working sixty to seventy hours a week to working twenty to thirty hours, and it felt strange. I felt like I had to stay busy and earn my keep. I couldn't possibly enjoy the day—that would be ridiculous.

As soon as Anthony stepped out the door each morning (I usually stayed at his house—oh, forgive me of my sins), I was abuzz, washing the dishes, changing the bed sheets, sweeping, vacuuming, and keeping the house tidy. My worth was completely and firmly tied to what I was doing rather than who I was.

But when Anthony caught on to my need to validate my being through constantly working, we started butting heads about it. I felt a constant need to prove that I was contributing to our household, yet he didn't quite see it that way. He kept telling me he had no interest in me as a housekeeper. *Hard to believe.*

One night, we were driving home from a pizza dinner, and I asked, "What *exactly* is my job, now that I have so much free time?" He took a second and said, "Your job is to be kind and thoughtful and fulfilled. Without those things, *our* world doesn't work." He added, "You took a leap of faith on us, and I honor that. You giving up a job where you worked long nights and odd hours enhances our lives, and for that I'm grateful."

Too good to be true? I was not a financial burden, and I did not have to earn my keep? I was enough?

Yes, I was enough.

Hope for Navigating—Taking a Leap

Sometimes we walk around with a ringing in our ears or a buzzing in our heads or a heaviness in our hearts telling us to make a move, but fear takes over and we suppress what's welling up inside. The only thing is, "We will never be able to escape our hearts. So it's better to listen to what they have to say."[1]

I loved Anthony and wanted a life with him, but I was not prepared for the inevitable questioning of my identity when I gave up the security, comradery, and freedom that went hand-in-hand with my music theatre job. I struggled to find my worth in my new normal.

Taking that leap made my stomach drop, but as fate would have it, I had been introduced to the feeling one year earlier. On a bright spring day, my girlfriend and I headed over to a local trapeze complex. Forty dollars was sure to get us a good time and, at the very least, some good photo ops. During the instructional portion, we were taught how to hook our knees around the wooden bar, how to chalk our hands and grab the bar, how to swing, and eventually, how to *let go* of the bar—in mid-swing, while we were upside down—and reach for our catcher. "NO HESITATION. When we say 'hands off,' LET GO."

I climbed up the ladder thirty feet, stayed firmly in position on the platform, and eventually grabbed the bar and aired out my wet armpits. I jumped off the platform and screamed as I felt the wall on the opposite side of the building coming toward my face. I swung in the air like a pendulum and fell onto the safety net. *Close but no cigar.*

But two months later, I returned and climbed the ladder again, knowing this time I was capable of reaching for the catcher. I felt a little less nervous while my toes curled over the tiny wooden platform and assumed the position. *Trust,* I told myself. I thrust my hips forward, bent my knees, and jumped off the platform. *TRUST.* As I was flying through the air,

I heard, "hands off;" I let go, reached out with conviction, and felt two strong arms grab mine. *YES.*

The leap I took leaving my job was the beginning of a new life that I could never have embraced without first letting go.

Droves of us are thinking about taking leaps in our lives. Fifty-one percent of Americans are dissatisfied with their jobs,[2] and in a study from National Opinion Research at the University of Chicago, results showed that in 2014 almost forty-nine percent of people felt their lives were routine or dull. Those numbers do not depict the rosiest of outlooks.

Taking a leap requires gumption. We may have thought about obvious pitfalls, but there is no real safety net. Taking a leap requires us to let go of what has given us comfort or power or security—in my case, all three—in order to open up a space for new things to unfold.

"A bird sitting on a tree is never afraid of the branch
breaking because her trust is not on the
branch but on her own wings."
—*unknown*

Trail Journal

2/26/18

Is there a situation in your life right now where you know you'd like to take a leap but are scared?

Writing a book

If you could wave a magic wand, what would you want your life to look like?

Writer
Speaker
preacher?
not wife

Mom
beloved

What are some ways you can start walking toward your magic wand life?

Put in the work, trusting results will come.

Chapter 3

ANXIETY

I was absolutely marriage material. I had left one of my jobs, and we were practically living together. *When was he going to propose?* My impatience was getting the best of me *and* the worst of me. We were a little less than a year in, and I had successfully honored kindness in a man (Thank you, Jesus!) and he in me (Thank you, Jesus!), ~~but I was radiating impatience.~~ I knew I loved him and he loved me, yet I was so *yep* knotted up that my conversations about marriage became desperately obvious. Marriage was of maximal importance to me and of minimal importance to Anthony. *Would he ever change his views?* It felt like I had been waiting an eternity. *And if we were to get engaged, how long before we were married? We weren't getting any younger!*

I clearly had extra time. "Idle hands are the devil's playground," as they say, so I started in on a health to-do list. It was a good time for me to visit with my holistic doctor and take control of my vices: alcohol, desserts … and well, alcohol and desserts. *hahaha*

During my visit, I told my doctor that I wanted to have children soon (cart WAY before the horse), and she suggested a course of action—mainly a sugar cleanse and prenatal vitamins. If and when I became pregnant, I wanted the egg to have the best possible landing spot. Never mind that we weren't even engaged yet. Did I mention that? I was preparing my body for a pregnancy that I hoped was around the corner.

During the sugar cleanse of 2012 (It was a life event), Anthony and I packed up our dogs—Beau Jackson and Mischa—and more luggage than we needed, and drove west to Alpine, Texas. The scenery was breathtaking. Smack dab in the middle of summer, the mountains were violet, the rolling hills lush green, and the morning air so crisp it seemed imported. We spent our time in West Texas hiking our way through Big Bend, driving to the Fort Davis Mountains, and listening to live music in historic hotels. It was perfectly slow. We cracked open paperbacks, played chess on our rented home patio, and swam in the deep blue Balmorhea Springs. I blogged, and he caught up on news. We had nowhere to go and nowhere to be. It was lovely.

One morning, Anthony suggested a hike. "Sure!" I responded, up for the challenge. It was before noon, and yet the sun shone brightly. Before we were even halfway up the mountain, I broke out in a sweat. Anthony suggesting a hike made me think he had something stirring, but I wasn't quite sure. *Could this be IT?* We continued hiking, negotiating the rocky trail, until we finally reached the top. We looked around for a flat boulder, took a seat, and gazed at the town. Alpine was beautiful and still—there was no traffic to contend with and no skyscrapers to peer over, just a small city nestled between mountains. We made small talk, and for a moment I thought—*This IS it! He's going to propose.*

But then, he didn't, and I realized I was wrong ... yet again. I was so excited about the possibility of his marriage proposal that I had conjured up scenarios before, only to be wrong time after time. Being wrong about it one more time wasn't *that* bad. Eventually I'd be right, I hoped. I'd be right, *right?*

We dusted off and headed back down the trail, admiring the wildlife and tiptoeing around cacti. About halfway down the trail, we walked onto a lookout.

"Let's stop here," he suggested.

We settled onto a boulder just big enough for both of us to sit on. And just when the conversation seemed to be running away from us, he went from sitting next to me to kneeling in front of me. *This was it! Or was it? Was it really happening? Yes, it was. Come back to your body, Catia. You're going to want to remember this.*

On bended knee, Anthony asked if I would do him the honor of being his wife, and with tears streaming down my cheeks, I answered, "Yes."

It happened!

Praise Jesus!

Shortly after our engagement, and while I was whipping wedding details together, my impatience got the better of me (yes, again), and I sought out a fertility specialist. I couldn't leave well enough alone. Ridiculous. I had the man of my dreams, I was planning the wedding of my dreams, and immediately I had to have the child of my dreams too. Lunacy. We knew we wanted children, so we made appointments for some exploratory tests to make sure both of us were in good shape.

The experience in the doctor's office was uncharted territory for us as a couple. There were all sorts of personal questions that Anthony and I had only briefly discussed, if the topics had even come up at all.

"Are you married?" the nurse asked.

"We will be," we said, as if we had to justify being there together.

"Have you been pregnant before? Have you had abortions? Have you fathered a child before? Do you do drugs?"

I told the truth, however uncomfortable it was. All I could think was—*I'm glad I've been honest with Anthony.* If I had had something to hide, the world would have caved in on me.

Afterward, the nurse shuffled us into an examination room and instructed me to undress from the waist down and to take a seat on the table. Moments later, a doctor introduced himself and began. My face flushed. My privates were being examined by a stranger and, to make matters worse, in front of Anthony! I covered my reddened face with my hands, as if that would relieve my embarrassment.

The doctor checked my reproductive organs from the inside. *Would we have a difficult time conceiving? Would my body pull through? Tell me, Doc!* As he looked at my ovaries, my fears subsided; it was clear that they were teeming with eggs! They were packed in so tightly that they looked like people inside an electronics store on Black Friday. Everything looked great, but the nurse also drew blood, just to make sure.

As we left, the medical staff reminded us that the average timetable for conception was a year.

"Great. We're in no rush," we responded.

But I absolutely was.

Just Between Us

I was out-of-my-mind impatient. My anxiety about the next moment and the next moment and the next moment caused me to miss the smells and sounds and tastes of the present moment. I was so obsessed with checking things off my life list that I worked myself into a tizzy. Just between us, it doesn't have to be that way.

Even in the midst of my anxiety, I had the sense, praise God, to try my best. From the start, I honored Anthony like we were going to be together forever. I often compared our relationship to an egg that I carried around with me, being ever so careful and ever so mindful not crack it. I believed treating our relationship with a high level of care would only make us stronger. I honored Anthony and, in return, he honored me. *Whoa!*

Thirty days after we were engaged, we were married. (I guess I sped up the process just a little.) On August 29, 2013, we had twenty-two of our closest friends and family members join us at what had been an old chapel in South Austin for an elegant outdoor Thursday afternoon wedding. It was as elegant as a wedding can be when it's a hundred degrees outside. Anthony still remembers (with fondness, of course!) how I pleaded with him to wear a tuxedo in the height of summer.

The words of Anthony's best friend, our officiant, seeped into my being and were written forever on our spirits as Anthony and I held each other's hands that day:

> Today you choose each other before God and your family and friends to begin your life together. Remember to treat yourselves and each other with respect, and remind yourselves often of what brought you together. Take responsibility for making the other feel safe, and give the highest priority to the tenderness, gentleness, and kindness that your connection deserves. When frustration, difficulty, and fear assail your relationship, as they threaten all relationships at some time or another, remember to focus on what is right between you, not just the part that seems wrong. In this way, you can survive the times when clouds drift across the face of the sun in your lives, remembering that, just because you may lose sight of it for a moment, does not mean the sun has gone

away. If each of you takes responsibility for the quality of your life together, it will be marked by abundance and delight. May you always need one another, not to fill emptiness, but to help each other know your fullness.

Now you will feel no rain, for each of you will be shelter for the other. Now you will feel no cold, for each of you will be warmth to the other. Now there will be no loneliness, for each of you will be companion to the other. Now you are two persons, but there is only one life before you. Now you will always have a safe place to call home. May beauty surround you both in the journey ahead, and through all the years, may happiness be your companion and your days together be good and long upon the earth."[3]

We cried through our personal vows, exchanged wedding bands, smooched in front of our loved ones, and were pronounced husband and wife. The keyboard player began playing Jackie Wilson's "Your Love Is Taking Me Higher," and as I wrapped my left arm into Anthony's body, we walked down the aisle together. I felt light. I felt free.

After all of my worrying, fretting, and list-making, it turned out my anxiety was pointless and could have possibly even ruined my relationship. I was like a rocking chair, always moving but never going anywhere. Come close and hear my words, dear friend: I know sometimes it seems impossible to do, but *trust the timing of your life.*

From time to time, you may find yourself doubting the way life is unfolding. I understand the craving to have it all play out *just* as you'd like. But you must learn to boldly trust the unfolding in order to experience your life in all its fullness. When you are worrying, you're missing out on RIGHT NOW. According to Proverbs 3:5, "Trust in the LORD with all thine heart; and lean not unto thine own understanding" (King James Version). All the pieces of your life are falling into place at *just* the right time.

Hope for Navigating—Anxiety

In *The Power of Now*, Eckhart Tolle teaches that we are not our thoughts and that the present moment holds the key to liberation. But we cannot find the present moment as long as we are stuck in our minds.

> *"When you dance, your purpose is not to get to a certain place on the floor. It's to enjoy each step along the way."*
> —Dr. Wayne Dyer

Our egos scream at us that one day we will be happy if _____. And no matter how fast we go or how high we climb, as soon as we reach our marker, our egos set their sights on the next horizon. Our egos reduce our present moments as a means to an end. And that leaves our minds in constant motion, perpetually exhausted. As Wayne Dyer says, "When you dance, your purpose is not to get to a certain place on the floor. It's to enjoy each step along the way."

When your mind begins to race and your heart starts to feel the weight of fear, you are either gripping onto the embers of your past mistakes, or your thoughts are reeling for a future that cannot be controlled. In order to get a hold of your anxiety, you must learn to become present.

When you feel anxiety about a relationship, job, or finances, get still and look around. Where are you? Are you safe? Maybe you have food available to you. Maybe you have warm shelter. Maybe you have a family at home who loves you. Maybe you have a dog who couldn't be happier you're home. Come back into your present fortunes and name them. Gently guide your mind out of the downward spiral of possibilities and back into the present. You, beloved, have the power to control your thoughts.

"Stress is caused by being HERE
but wanting to be THERE."
–Eckhart Tolle

Trail Journal

Do you have anxious thoughts and episodes?

Sometimes.

Less + less frequently!

Is there something you long for in the future?

Hopes for then, but also happiness for now

How will you practice embracing the present moment?

Stay here, now.

Chapter 4

VULNERABILITY

A few weeks after our wedding, we were blissfully sauntering around Barcelona. Our honeymoon had begun. The sun lit up the sandy beaches, the centuries-old architecture stood proudly, and Gaudí's works delighted. We ate grilled calamari beachside, sunned ourselves next to topless locals, and ate more *jamón serrano* than I thought possible. I loved how the ladies seemed beautiful and yet soft, forgetting to subscribe to gyms. I relished the late-night meals, and I loved the chic surroundings.

A few evenings into our trip, Anthony received a call from our fertility clinic but kept our blood test results to himself until my jet lag had worn off. As we were dressing for a day of sightseeing, Anthony finally relayed the information. "I tested positive for two out of a thousand gene mutations, and you tested positive for one out of a thousand gene mutations."

I suspended any thought, unconsciously holding my breath.

"And one of my positives and your positive match." Silence settled in the room. "Our match means that, if you were able to carry a pregnancy to term, our child would have a 25 percent chance of dying before their first birthday, and the majority of that year would be spent in critical care."

I couldn't believe what I was hearing. *How was this possible?*

"What?" I responded incredulously. "But I'm *completely* healthy, and you are *completely* healthy. Not survive?" I was stunned. "NOT SURVIVE!?"

I couldn't wrap my mind around the notion that even though Anthony and I were healthy, our future offspring might not have a chance of survival. My body was in Spain, but I may as well have been in a cave. My thoughts ran away from me, and my heart grew heavy. I couldn't figure out why the results turned out the way they did. *Had I done something wrong?* And even though I heard "25 percent," I wasn't sure what it all meant. I fell into a hole and felt sorry for myself and for us. Would I be unable to conceive a healthy baby without scientific intervention? Would we have to do IVF? What even *was* IVF?

That day, I moped around Barcelona's cobblestone streets. I fed my feelings with creamy gelato, roamed in circles, and finally found the Basílica of Santa Maria del Mar. It was blocks from the ocean, and the 600-year-old building smelled of wet wood and salt, its pews more welcoming because of the warm ocean air. I paced the interior of the church, paying homage to each saint and their respective altars. I needed to pray, so I slid into a pew and knelt. *Lord, please give me the strength, grace, and courage to get through this. I need your help. I know this is happening for a reason, and I know I am strong enough to handle it. But I need your help and guidance to get through this. I need your mercy.* I knelt in silence until there was a dull ache in my knees. I stood, massaged them, and headed toward the back of the basilica where the gift shop was located. I took out my coin purse and purchased a prayer candle and a locally made wooden rosary. With my new rosary as armor, I stopped in front of the main altar, knelt on my left knee, and took in one more breath. *In the name of the Father, and of the Son, and of the Holy Spirit. Amen.*

The day after we learned the terrible news, we walked out of Gaudí's La Sagrada Família, and I saw a kiosk selling soccer tickets. If we could score some tickets, I knew that Anthony's experience in Spain would be much more memorable, and maybe I'd be able to get my mind off the bad news. We walked up to the kiosk, chatted with the attendant, and to our surprise, Barca was slated for a home game later that night! We jumped at the chance to purchase tickets. What a score! Anthony's day was made, which meant mine was made too.

The energy inside the stadium was electrifying, and our seats were top-notch, next to the owner's box! The field was a perfectly manicured electric green, the players chiseled, and the fans unable to be quelled. Camp Nou trembled with cheers. Lionel Messi, the star himself, scored on a header, and Barca won handily. It was a Tuesday for the books. Amped up from the night win, we stopped at a tiny shop serving cappuccino and pizza and grabbed a seat at one of their sidewalk tables. We had each had a wonderful day, were well-rested, and somehow knew we were ready to talk about the genetic testing results.

I began. "What exactly do the results mean?"

Anthony explained that we were both recessive carriers of CDG1-A. If our baby acquired both our recessive genes, it was possible he or she would not survive past the first year, and the situation would be traumatic. He reiterated that there was only a 25 percent chance of this worst-case scenario where both our recessive genes would be passed on to our child. All other scenarios would, in fact, be just fine. If we proceeded naturally, we were rolling the dice and hoping to fall in the 75 percent.

As we sipped on our chocolate-sprinkled cappuccinos and discussed the possibilities, I couldn't help but think, *I haven't had my period in a few weeks. What if I'm pregnant right now? What will that mean? Will I have to get an abortion?* And then I said it out loud. "If I'm pregnant now and the baby has this, I am willing to terminate the pregnancy." I hoped God would forgive me for being so cavalier, and I also hoped God would understand. We concluded that we did not want to be terminating pregnancies willy-nilly, as neither of us was built for that sort of emotional pull. We only had bits of information, but what we knew about CDG1-A absolutely scared us. Sitting there at eleven o'clock on a

Barcelona sidewalk, I was unsure if I wanted to be pregnant or not. The dream that I had of a fairytale conception was whisked away.

With this new information and what it potentially meant for our experience of parenthood, my period being a few weeks late sat differently with me. I was no longer excited; I was full of dread. We wrapped up our time in Barcelona and headed to Germany. And with each passing day, my anxiety about being late increased.

Germany was surprisingly pleasant. It wasn't as *German* as I thought it would be. The weather was cold, and the skies grey, but the scenery more than made up for it. We stayed with wonderful friends who lived as Europeans (i.e., efficiently). We cycled through Munich and filled our bellies with pig knuckle from street vendors. We braved Oktoberfest with my brother David and sister-in-law Gabby (who happened to be in Germany at the time), and we even rented a car and drove south through the countryside to Schwangau, home of the world-renowned Neuschwanstein Castle.

Before heading out, we stopped at a local grocery store. I needed a pregnancy test. I was more than two weeks late, and with every passing day I was *more than two weeks late.* I had to be pregnant … I just had to be! But I could not, for the life of me, find a pregnancy test in Germany.

We arrived in Schwangau, and a valet ushered us into a romantic room. The bay window looked straight onto Neuschwanstein. It was the view of which Hollywood honeymoons are made. As I was unpacking, I pulled out some black lace lingerie I had stowed away. Surely, that would lift our spirits! There was only one small problem—first I'd have to overcome my heart-stopping fear of lingerie and of initiating sex.

When I was single, I pretended to be made of stone. I pretended that being rejected by someone didn't hurt, but it always did, and I hated it. I wanted so badly to be flippant, callous, and unattached, but I always failed miserably. Vulnerability made me uncomfortable because there was

ALWAYS the possibility I would get hurt. I was eager for the day when I was a wife, and fear saw itself out of my life. Obviously, I would not be vulnerable once happily settled.

WRONG. I was hitched and still afraid of rejection! Damn. I was married but still nervous about initiating sex with my husband! Was I the only wife that felt this way? And I was absolutely terrified of initiating sex by walking out in lingerie. Double whammy! What was I thinking? I bombarded myself with pointless questions: *What shoes should I wear? Should I even wear shoes? How should I walk out? Before drinks? After drinks? If I was really pregnant, should I be drinking?* hahahahaha

In the movies, it always plays out so perfectly. The lighting is just right. Neither person has had too much for dinner. The woman is completely confident in her scanty attire. She walks into the bedroom ever so slowly, and the man is always pleased and raring to go. No glitches. *When I tiptoed out, would Anthony be shocked, or would he giggle? Would he be too tired? Would I even look good? Would I be attractive enough?* It was easier to wrangle snakes than wrangle my thoughts. *Get it together! The time will never be better.*

I tucked my black lace lingerie into my hands and walked into the bathroom, Anthony none the wiser. I freshened up, and then I stalled. My heart started to race, and my palms began to sweat. *No, I won't do it. No harm, no foul. I had never promised lingerie anyway. Yes, yes, I have to do it. No, no, I don't. What does it mean that I don't feel comfortable initiating sex? Yes, yes, I must do it.* I stared in the mirror for a few minutes and gave myself a pep talk. *You'll be fine. You can do this. He loves you. He will not laugh at you.*

I opened the bathroom door, took a few steps out (no shoes), got Anthony's attention, and almost immediately started crying. *Shoot.* I had so much pent-up anxiety! I admitted my nervousness and that I had been working up the courage for months. He held me close, told me he loved me, and reassured me that I had nothing to worry about. And then ... you know. It all turned out *just right*! *Hallelujah!*

As soon we were back in the States, I made an appointment with my OB/GYN's office to see if I was, in fact, pregnant. But—I wasn't. I was sad, and then taken aback that I was sad. *Why be sad?* A negative result meant that everything was fine. I would not have to abort a baby. This was good news! Or was it? I wasn't sure what I wanted.

A month later, we continued our travels, packing our brightest bathing suits and most comfortable flip-flops. Costa Rica or bust! As I packed for the trip, I came across Brené Brown's book, *The Gifts of Imperfection,* and added it to my suitcase.

On our first full day there, I wanted to surf in the Pacific. The water was inviting, the waves looked manageable, and I was excited about the experience. My optimism was unbridled, even though I had only surfed once. "No lesson for me, thanks." With board in hand, I made my way to the water.

Hmmm ... this surfboard is awful hard to balance on, even on my belly. Agh! No big deal. It'll just take a few minutes for my muscle memory to kick in. That never happened. I tried and tried and tried. I knew I was doing several things wrong, and I wasn't able to get it together. I was pissed that I was getting pounded by the ocean. My eyes burned from the salt water, and my hair was a mess. Every time I went down off the board, my bathing suit rolled up, and I'd have to readjust. I was blowing snot left and right. A *lot* of energy was being expended. It was a battle with the saltwater, and the saltwater was winning, 45–1. Anthony offered help, but I wouldn't take it. Surfing was not going well. I thought it wise to pause for lunch and then head back out alone. I was not going to be defeated.

Once I was alone, I realized I was falling more, but I was also giving it a little more gusto, not so worried about my hair and bathing suit, or looking silly. I even willed myself up on a few of the waves. After about

hahaha!

fifteen minutes on my mission impossible, a local said, "It's nice to see someone so dedicated." *Ok, at least I'm getting a gold star for something.* He offered me some tips about being decisive and foot placement, and *bam!* I was up and felt like a million bucks. When Anthony scooped me up, we shared in my newfound happiness earned by my willingness to try.

Later that afternoon, I picked up *The Gifts of Imperfection*:

> The comparison mandate becomes this crushing paradox of "fit in and stand out." It's be like everyone else, but better. Comparison is not a to-do list item. For most of us, it's something that requires constant awareness. Creativity helps us stay mindful that what we bring to the world is completely original. Risk feeling vulnerable and new and imperfect. Try something that scares you or something you've dreamt about trying.[4]

Yeah

Those powerful words made me realize that if I didn't compare myself to others, I took away my own ammunition: *I would have nothing with which to berate myself.* There would be no one to consider myself "less than." My anxiety dam released, and the tears rushed out in a torrent.

I found Anthony, spilled the beans, and hugged it out with him. He told me that this was all part of a partnership and that he loved me for moments like *this* (moments of growth and introspection and self-awareness), not for my surfer girl potential. "Thank God! I can bring you moments like this *all day long* because … this is me!"

Me too.

Just Between Us

Between our genetic testing results and learning to overcome my fear of putting myself out there, the first few months of our marriage were a master's course in vulnerability.

When I learned our genetic testing results, I was stunned and terrified. Immediately, it was all out of my control. I had planned a fairytale, and the results threw a wrench into it. *Didn't they get the memo?* I had devoted myself to being kind and honoring Anthony, but when the results came back, my ability to be kind and composed was tested. Could I stay steady when the world around me was twisting and turning? Could I find my center and keep it? I was in a new marriage, and every surprise that came my way posed an opportunity to continue proving to God that I could honor his blessings.

COME ON!

> "*Who you are in the fire is who you are.*"
> —Lisa Bevere

When we were in Germany and balancing the romance of a honeymoon with the test results, I really was doing my best. It was a huge step for me to initiate sex in lacy lingerie. I was saying, "Here I am. I love you, so let's enjoy each other." Just between us, it was terrifying, but I did it and bristled with confident vitality. With round-the-clock media showing us airbrushed versions of women that have full beauty teams, slipping on lingerie and feeling good about it is not easy! I also lived in fear of disappointing my husband because I wasn't an immediate success at everything I tried. It was uncomfortable to feel raw, exposed, and unsure. I wrestled plenty with vulnerability while on my own, but when I was vulnerable in front of the love of my life, it sent me into high-level anxiety.

Thankfully, Dr. Brene Brown's book taught me that feeling vulnerable isn't a bad thing! In fact, it's a sign of courage. When I was able to say, "This is who I am, and this is what I'm feeling," our marriage was all the better for it. In living honestly, our relationships grow deeper roots.

This vulnerability was awkward at first, and it continues to be years later, but I do it because … what's the alternative? Less emotion? No, thank you. Coming across Dr. Brené Brown's book just before our Costa Rica trip was a gift from God, as all things are. Please sit for this and hear me: gifts come from God every day, in all sorts of forms. Keep your eyes open and your ears peeled. He could be talking to you right now.

**In living honestly,
our relationships grow deeper roots.**

A key

Thankfully, I trusted my husband to handle me with care during my moments of heightened vulnerability. It is a spectacular quality to be trustworthy in those delicate moments. If you can sit with your partner's insecurities, hold them close, and treat them with care and tenderness, then you are a heart for the ages. And, if over time, you can learn how to accept your own wounds and insecurities, hold them close, and treat them with care and tenderness, then you'll be *unstoppable*.

Hope for Navigating—Being Vulnerable

Servant leadership is vulnerable

Bolstered by the connection I felt with Dr. Brene Brown's *The Gifts of Imperfection* and acknowledging how much it changed my life, I could not wait to devour her book on vulnerability entitled *Daring Greatly*. In it, she notes that the word *vulnerable* comes from the Latin "vulnerare," meaning *to wound*. Being vulnerable literally means that you are opening yourself up to be wounded. But why would we want to do that? Because that sense of openness is the crux of all things magnificent and deeply moving. Walking vulnerably is the only way to get from where we are to where we most want to be. *by nature.*

Brown notes how we love seeing raw truth and openness in other people, but we're afraid to let them see it in us, fearing that our truth isn't enough.[5] Yet how many times have we read a blog post or book, nodding the entire time, heart welling up with a feeling of acceptance, a sense of belonging, and a realization that we are not alone? What about that sense of relief we feel when a friend shares her own shortcomings or seeming failures that mirror our own?

Dr. Brown goes on to say in *Daring Greatly* that our ultimate struggle is wanting to experience someone's vulnerability but not wanting to be vulnerable ourselves.

If we are afraid to open ourselves to vulnerability, we are denying ourselves the fullness of the shared human existence and the deliciously warm feeling of belonging. Being vulnerable and sharing our whole selves then—shortcomings and failures and all—is not a sign of weakness, but a sign of strength.

How many times in our lives have we not really given something our best because we needed an excuse just in case we failed? *Well, I really didn't try my hardest. So I really didn't fail.* We are so intensely afraid to lose, not realizing that the winning and losing paradigm is an illusion. The question should not be, "Did we win or lose?" Instead, the question should be, "What did we try?" Winning and losing creates a sort of stagnation, while an attitude of trying creates a life of growth and movement and heightened vitality.

If we are afraid to open ourselves to
vulnerability, we are denying ourselves the
fullness of the shared human existence and the
deliciously warm feeling of belonging.

Let's ditch the idea of winning and losing in favor of a *trying* mentality. Instead of fearing vulnerability, let's practice *daring greatly*. If we want to feel deep love, exuberant joy, electricity running through our veins, life-saving grace, and a true connection with those around us, let's allow ourselves be fully seen.

"Vulnerability is not about fear and grief and disappointment.
It is the birthplace of everything we're hungry for."
—*Brené Brown*

Trail Journal

What makes you feel vulnerable?

Failure, losing control, not being good at something? betray + rejection.

Are there things in your life that you are unwilling to share with people? Why?

My heart usually. People have mistreated it before! But I need a new script. And then a new truth will emerge from the new script — "I can handle being seen, People love me."

How do you feel about the idea that trying is more important than winning or losing?

Resilience, Courage. All developed in the resistance — the battle.

Bob Goff says, "love makes us both strong and weak!"

Chapter 5

MARRIAGE IS ONLY MARRIAGE

I always knew I wanted to mother children, but I wasn't sure what that looked like. *Would I have children of my own? Would I adopt? Would I marry a man who already had children? Would I be like Oprah and open a school for children, and would they call me Mama C?* *hahaha*

After I knew I loved Anthony, but before *he* knew I loved him, he mentioned wanting to be a father, and—over crudités—the goal-setter in me did the math. I was twenty-nine, and he was thirty-nine. Assuming it *all* worked out, time wasn't exactly on our side. I knew we had a long road ahead before the subject of children was broached, but I imagined it anyway.

I wanted children *someday*, but I thought he wanted them *right away*, so I circled back to the idea of children in conversation with him, again and again. Desperate, I wanted him to know I was ready; rather, I was ready to be with him, but I didn't know if I was ready for children. I was all about making his dreams come true: "Here, take this baby as a token of my love for you." *hahaha*

It all seemed grand … until I thought about what would happen if I weren't able to deliver, and that prospect seemed like a nightmare. *What*

under promise / over deliver

if I made promises I couldn't keep? If I ultimately couldn't have children for Anthony ... would he still value me?

My presumptions about having children were off the charts. I was betting the house on being a young, fertile, Mexican woman. I thought we should act speedily; our window of opportunity was closing. I wanted it all, and I wanted it right away. *Girl, Me too.*

Our possible pregnancy was the bone I chewed on for months. *Am I pregnant? How about now? Today? Maybe now? Nope, not yet. I missed my birth control by four hours, so how about today?* I'll bet I took fifteen pregnancy tests in the span of six months. It was total lunacy.

And all of this was WAY before the fertility center called with our genetic testing results. I worked myself into a tizzy before there was even one obstacle in the way. When an obstacle did present itself and I had to contend with truth, my stress climbed to the next level. *Would Anthony still love me? If I couldn't give him children, would he be heartbroken? Would our marriage be as strong?*

I had heard infertility horror stories—stories of couples spending years and years and tens of thousands of dollars trying to conceive ... but not every couple living happily ever after. Some were able to conceive, and some weren't. And some of the marriages were worse off because of the constant pressure. I did not want my new marriage to bear that weight, even with the looming genetic testing results; I wanted to let it all go, but I couldn't quite do it. I was worried, and I wanted a plan.

What would we do? Would we roll the dice, or would we do IVF? My mind swirled for weeks, my spirit wound so tightly. I tensed up so much that my husband and I had to talk about it.

He told me that he had married me for *me*, not for my ability to bear children. He told me that when couples enter into marriage, their only promise is to have each other, and sometimes even that doesn't happen.

He told me he hoped to have children with me but that he didn't expect it. And he told me that whatever the case, we would have each other.

As I sat with his kindness, I felt monumentally relieved. All this time, I had assigned children as his priority. Children weren't; *I was*. I felt wonderful and ridiculous all at the same time. The story I created was happening entirely inside *my* head: my ego and insecurities were the only participants. I desperately wanted to manage the when, where, why, what, and how, but I finally realized I couldn't control any of it. After that gift of a conversation, we put it out of our minds and enjoyed each other. And this time, we succeeded. *yep!*

> **The story I created was happening entirely inside *my* head: my ego and insecurities were the only participants. I desperately wanted to manage the when, where, why, what, and how, but I finally realized I couldn't control any of it.**

Just Between Us

I wanted to fulfill Anthony's dreams. I told him how much I loved him, but I wanted to *show* him. "Giving" him children was how you did it, I thought. Children were a gift I could bring to the table of our relationship. And although my motive came from a place of kindness, it was out of line. Children change the layout of our lives in the most major way, and I was sweeping that truth under the rug. I was only focused on the romance of it all.

After stressing about a possible pregnancy in the hypothetical and then in actuality, I realized that I was playing with house money. The promise of children was NEVER mine to make, nor would it ever be. Becoming pregnant was not ultimately up to me—it was up to God.

After wrestling with it, I settled into the notion that *I* was plenty. I was the gift I brought to the table of our relationship. I was worth being with because of my character, my kindness, and my thoughtfulness. I was worth loving all on my own, unadorned. And that was a relief, but also terrifying. For so long, I had relied on what I could do for others as a form of power. I used what I could do for others as a crutch, a way to prove my worthiness.

Just between us, marriage isn't a promise of happily ever after. It's a union of friends, a union of partners, a union of two souls who enter into adventures (both good *and* not so good) together. And despite (and maybe because of) the twists and turns, marriage can be the best adventure of your life. If a marriage is a happily ever *effort*, the happily ever after falls into place.

Hope for Navigating—Marriage

The infamous line in *Jerry Maguire*, "You complete me," really did a lot of us in. It made an entire generation of folks feel like two people made a whole. And it sent us all in search of our other half—in search of someone who would fly cross-country on a whim and burst into our living room, confessing with all the passion of a Richard Burton-Elizabeth Taylor relationship, that WE completed them!

But the movie we were watching was fiction, and the lives we are living are non-fiction.

In *Lies at the Altar: The Truth About Great Marriages*, Dr. Robin L. Smith writes, "Two separate and fully alive individuals can agree to travel the same path together. It is with the assistance and cooperation of this steady relationship anchor that you can be a whole individual who can fully and freely offer another individual a place of shelter, rest, growth, and joy in a union that is primed to thrive."[6] In a nutshell, Jerry was wrong.

As our marriage deepened, Anthony and I started carefully revealing the rawest parts of our wounds and hearts. And each time the reveal was met with love and tenderness, our trust for each other grew. Additionally, every time Anthony honored my old wounds and beliefs and hopes for the future, I was able to move from a childish version of love to a more mature love. I no longer felt the need for constant validation, I no longer feared not being good enough, and I no longer feared the unknown between us. Over time, I transformed into a whole, capable person, sturdy in the conviction that *I* would always be okay, and *we* would always be okay.

A thriving marriage is built, in part, by honoring the trust your partner has placed in you, decision by decision. In the way the sun warms the earth during the day and the moon lights the earth at night, so should a marriage be—a constant and consistent cycle of thoughtfulness, kindness, gratitude, and acts of love.

A thriving marriage is built, in part, by honoring the trust your partner has placed in you, decision by decision.

"Marriage has the power to set the course of your life as a whole. If your marriage is strong, even if all the circumstances in your life around you are filled with trouble and weakness, it won't matter.
You will be able to move out into the world in strength."
—Tim Keller

Trail Journal

Are you afraid your partner won't love you if _____?

If I do less

How does being trusting or guarded affect your relationships?

Massively — It adds to my feeling of violation

Do you feel like a whole person, or are you hoping for a better half?

A whole, fully leaning on the Lord,

Chapter 6

LETTING GO

When I left my music theatre job in June of 2013, I was wary of being financially dependent on my then boyfriend. At thirty years old, I had carved out a nice life for myself. I had worked hard, gone to college, received a master's degree, worked harder, and thoroughly enjoyed my freedom and independence. When I left my job, my income was cut in half. Half! And I would get knots in my stomach thinking about what would happen to me if we broke up. *Where would that leave me financially?* I suspected that if I left the music theatre *and* moved in with my boyfriend, I would feel constricted. It was too much change without a safety net. So, like a big girl, I used my words and spoke up.

I admitted to my hesitance, and we extended the lease on my apartment until November 2013. If pigs started to fly and we broke up, I would not be out on the street; I'd have my apartment. Extending my lease was 99 percent mental. Just knowing I had my bases covered helped me sleep better at night.

Keeping my apartment also afforded me my own space (storage for most of my belongings) and a quiet place to write. It even served as a guesthouse of sorts. When friends and family visited, they always had a place to stay.

I only visited my apartment once in a while, but it was wonderful knowing I had a safety net—and more importantly, it brought me relief knowing that my boyfriend cared so much about me that he was willing to do something out of the ordinary.

If you are doing the math, we were engaged and married before the lease on my apartment was up! We were married, and I still had an apartment. It wasn't until late November, three months after we were married, that we officially moved in together.

I packed and purged, ever thoughtful about which belongings I wanted to bring into our communal space. I gave away all sorts of things that evoked memories from loves past, or from traumas past. I wanted everything I brought into our space to be joyful and peaceful. I didn't want any of my sullied stories following me. It was an opportunity for a clean slate, and I seized it.

Just Between Us

Taking a little extra time to meld belongings allowed us to focus on each other rather than debating whose coffee table we would use. There were no fights about whose paintings we'd keep, or whose sofas would *have* to be given away. There were some things I loved that he abhorred and vice versa, so we made space for each other's preferences. Marriage is an adventure, remember? We have now been married a few years, and we still haven't quite found our collective style. But we're getting there!

Life is dynamic and more joyful when we can grow and stretch along the way. It took time and willingness, but eventually I moved from a place of fear to a place of letting go.

From time to time, fear bubbles up inside because we are worried about not fitting in, not living our lives the way our parents would have us live them, or not gaining the approval of someone we love—sometimes even someone we don't really care for! What stops us from being happy is the image of what we think we "should" look like.

Just between us, your life doesn't always have to look like you thought it would. It doesn't have to look like what others think it should look like either. It's okay to be honest about who you are and what you need. It's your life, and what a privilege it is to get to design every bit of it.

It's okay to be honest about who you are and what you need. It's your life, and what a privilege it is to get to design every bit of it.

Hope for Navigating—Letting Go

In my mid-twenties, I participated in a volcanic eruption of a break-up. The layers and layers of wounds were raw for years. Upon breaking up, I moved out of the home we shared and back into my childhood home with my parents. My life had unraveled, and I had perceived my starting anew as a step back when, in reality, it was the beginning of stepping into my power. After I had had my share of wallowing and when I was ready, I cracked open the book, *Feel the Fear and Do It Anyway* by Dr. Susan Jeffers. Jeffers taught me how to walk with fear; fear did not have to be a barrier to my success. She taught me that, in fact, I could feel the fear and channel it.

A suggested exercise in her book is to recite empowering statements as a way to rescript one's mind. My interior life was in such disarray that I recited these truths twenty-five times, three times a day. I repeated them while I drove to work, while I showered, and while I cooked over the stove. I did it for four months straight, and it changed the underpinnings of my mind.

Five truths about fear:[7]

1. The fear will never go away as long as I continue to grow.
2. The only way to get rid of the fear of doing something is to go out and do it.

3.   The only way to feel better about myself is to go out and do it.
4.   Not only am I going to experience fear when I'm on unfamiliar territory, so is everybody else.
5.   Pushing through fear is less frightening than living with the underlying fear that comes from a feeling of helplessness.

Rescripting the tapes in my mind moved me from a position of pain to a position of power. And when it came time for me to let go of my apartment, my safe space, I tapped back into what I had learned years earlier and reminded myself that I could handle whatever came my way. I traded the paralysis of fear for the peace and joy of letting go.

When there is something we know we need to let go of, we would do well to pay attention to the chatter box inside our minds. While humans can speak 200-300 words per minute, our subconscious speaks at up to 1,000 words per minute. The subconscious mind is 88 percent of the brain's capacity and does not work on logic, only on what it is fed.[8] When we need to let go of a career, a relationship, or a mind-set, instead of focusing on our fears, let's focus on our strengths, our power. However corny or cumbersome, rescripting our thoughts can be just what we need.

Rescripting the tapes in my mind moved me from a position of pain to a position of power.

"There is no illusion greater than fear."
—Lao Tzu

48

Trail Journal

3/1/18

What is something you are afraid of?

Losing control.

WHY are you afraid of it?

Because I have lost control before.

Are you willing to move through the fear?

Yes. Movement is healing. When I choose to move, I choose my own healing.

Chapter 7

HOLIDAY CHANGES

First comes love, then comes marriage, and then comes the division of holidays.

We spent our first Thanksgiving as a married couple in Austin. We enjoyed a long, delightful lunch with close friends, and in the evening, we bundled up and cheered the University of Texas (UT) Longhorns football team to victory. It was a perfectly entertaining day, but my first Thanksgiving Day as a wife was entirely different than every other I had experienced before.

Midafternoon, something in me switched, and I was not in the best of moods. I was irritated. *What happened?* I wanted to wag my moody finger in someone's or something's direction. The scavenger hunt began. *Anthony was acting funny. Yeah, that's it! Anthony is acting funny.* Nope. Okay, next corner. Maybe the weather was the culprit. *I'm freezing and uncomfortable. Yes, that's got to be it!* I was cold, but, after a quick check, overall I was fine. Nope. Try again. *I'm hungry, and there are no more corn dogs left in the entire stadium! How can corn dogs be 86'd at a college football game? Who does the inventory around here?!* I muscled through the football game and swayed back and forth when the band played a fun song, but I felt crummy and was having a hard time shaking it. I couldn't quite tell what was wrong; my mood was heavy, sullen even.

When we got home from the game and took off our cold-weather boots, Anthony looked at me and said, "I think you're sad you're not home."

The wheels in my head turned, but I remained quiet.

As I surveyed the day, I realized I had had very little interaction with my family. My dad and I exchanged some texts and pictures. (He impressively upped his turkey-carving skills with the help of YouTube.) And I had only spoken with my mom for a few minutes early in the day. Normally, my folks host Thanksgiving lunch for all my aunts, uncles, and cousins. Most years, there are about forty people in the house, and when they all hold hands and bow their heads for grace, I know it's not only a unifying family moment, but also one that my late Grandma and Grandpa would be proud of.

They called and put me on speakerphone while grace was being said so I could bow my head with them in prayer—which was nice, but it felt like crumbs. As I continued to think, it dawned on me that I hadn't talked to my brothers, *and* I hadn't eaten my Grandma's rice recipe that had been handed down through the years. I hadn't laughed with any of my cousins … I hadn't been *home*. I quickly sent my brothers a sentimental email, and I realized just how much being with my family during the holidays meant to me.

Just Between Us

All my life, I had celebrated major holidays with my family, and I knew that becoming a wife would change that, but I didn't know exactly how. I knew that holidays would be divided, but I didn't anticipate a little hole in my heart because of the change of pace. My Thanksgiving in Austin was delightful, and luckily, I spent it with the man I love. But it was entirely different from the thirty previous Thanksgiving days.

So many times, we don't even stop to recognize how much we love someone or something until it goes away, until it's no longer at our

yeah. Me too girl.

fingertips. Just between us, I thought I had a good handle on gratitude and being in the moment. I thought everyone else was taking things for granted. Certainly *I* wasn't taking things for granted! But I was. As we age and grow and take on new responsibilities and relationships, our lives take different shapes. Things won't always be the way they "were." And would we really want that anyway?

When I married Anthony, I promised to build a life *with* him, not simply *Yes.* invite him into *my* life. Does that make sense? With this change, there was a tinge of sadness because I loved *my* life, but it was only mine, not ours.

It involves both of us.

So, after pouting for a little bit, I resolved that it was okay to embrace the change and grieve the loss of my familiar holiday structure. It was okay that we didn't spend 4.3 hours with my family and 4.3 hours with his, like the rule book said we should. WE were the new family. It was a wonderful, yet monumental, change.

Change sheds light. That's why it's often painful, often wholesome.

When I married Anthony, I promised to build a life *with* him, not simply invite him into *my* life.

Hope for Navigating—Holidays and Change

Change is hard, even when it's a good change, because it usually brings with it a sense of loss and consequently, grief. We instinctively hold onto the things that are safe and comfortable, and we shy away from the unknown. English philosopher Alan Watts encourages, "The only way to make sense out of change is to plunge into it, move with it, and join the dance." Doesn't that make you want to drink a glass of wine with dear ole' Alan? *Yep!*

By definition, we are changing. Harvard psychologist Dan Gilbert said in his TEDtalk, "Human beings are works in progress that mistakenly think they're finished. We all know we will change, but we think, fundamentally, the people we've become … will remain relatively stable in the future. And in that, we are wrong." *Wrong?*

Think of how much we have changed since childhood, since our teenage years, or since being young adults. Each new stage of life brings about a shift in circumstances, perspectives, and even preferences. If we expect *embrace* change, however, it will be less likely to derail us when it inevitably occurs. *amen*

Change is, by definition, a form of loss, but change can also be good— great even! Change means we're stretching beyond our status quo. Change means we have the opportunity to understand ourselves at a deeper level. Change means we're willing to flex as we receive new information. And if we're changing, we're alive—what a gift.

Change means we have the opportunity to understand ourselves at a deeper level.

We each face big changes in our lives. Perhaps we are navigating a new relationship and mourning the loss of "the way things were," or we are watching our children grow into young men and women. Or maybe we are moving to a new city, starting life again on our own, or coping with the loss of a loved one. Whatever the case and however heart-wrenching, we get to decide how we are going to handle that change.

"To be fully alive, fully human, and completely awake is to be continually thrown out of the nest."
—*Pema Chödrön*

love this so much!

Trail Journal

Does change excite you or bother you?

Both. :) When I am healthy, I welcome it readily.

What changes are you facing in your life right now?

Downsizing our commitments to make space for kids. :)

What is one way you can "plunge into change, move with it, and join the dance"?

Engage, improv skills. Say thanks. :)

Chapter 8

POSITIVE PREGNANCY

We were headed to the Galapagos for the New Year's holiday. *Fancy.* And to take advantage of the Galapagos Islands' beauty, my husband and I signed up for private scuba diving lessons at a local Austin shop. With a scuba diving certification, we'd be able to see all of what the Galapagos had to offer.

On a cold and dreary Saturday in November, we headed to the scuba shop. I dreaded the idea of scuba diving. Big open sea, lack of control, *no thank you.* But I wanted to be supportive—enthusiastic even—about my husband's hobbies, so I agreed to take part. *hahahahaha!*

As we piddled around the shop, the staff advised us on gear and scheduling and handed us forms, including health waivers, to fill out. They told us we needed to be cleared by a doctor in case there were any outstanding conditions that would prevent us from having safe diving experiences. "Are you pregnant?" the associate asked, in passing.

"No, sir, sure not."

"Ok, great. Just confirm that and then sign this waiver." He explained that scuba diving posed risks for babies in the womb.

Anthony and I paid for our nonrefundable private lessons and enjoyed the rest of our Saturday afternoon. The next day, December 1, after turkey club sandwiches for lunch, I prepared for scuba class. I took out the materials and spread them over the kitchen table. I flipped through the timer instruction manual, and that alone made me woozy. But then I saw the health waiver, and I thought I'd take care of the confirmation.

I still had a few pregnancy tests stored under my bathroom sink from my overly anxious days, so I quietly took one. I sat on top of the toilet, waiting, just as I had done so many times before, my hopes neutral. I sat there in my worn jeans and stared at the stick—*negative, negative, negative.* But as the seconds passed, a bright pink line started to show on the left side of the results window. I had taken enough tests to know that the pink line indicating NO was at the *right* side of the results window. A minute and a half had gone by. My interest piqued as I continued to stare at the stick, and to my everlasting surprise, ANOTHER pink line appeared. *Two pink lines, two pink lines.* I grabbed the box and read the instructions. "Two pink lines indicate pregnancy." I looked at the test. Two pink lines. I looked at the instructions. Two pink lines: PREGNANT. PREGNANT.

PREGNANT?! HOLY … !

For a few minutes, the information was ALL mine. I sat in amazement. *Were we really pregnant? Was I with child?*

I stood up and walked the twenty-five feet to the patio where Anthony was relaxing in the hammock, catching up on the day's newspapers. He had no clue.

"Honey," I said, with some quiver in my voice, "I took a pregnancy test."

His head peeked out of the right side of his paper. "Yes?"

"And it says I'm pregnant."

Then—a pause to end all pauses.

"Good," his voice cracked.

"Good? Good?" *I obviously was looking for a little more enthusiasm.* "How did this happen?" Rhetorical.

"Well, that's what happens when you have unprotected sex." His literal ways are never to be outdone! "Well, Catia, do you have another pregnancy test? Would you like to take it?"

I did. Pregnant! My legs wobbled. *Could I really be?* Filled with nervous energy, I paced around the house, and my goal-oriented self kicked in. I wanted to be far enough along to feel secure in the positive test result. I had a new compulsive mission. I drove to the pharmacy and picked up a more detailed pregnancy test, one that told me how far along I was. The results: four to six weeks. *Yes! Four to six weeks!* That evening, my head hit the pillow without me drinking my Sunday evening nightcap.

The next day, I woke up determined to get an official medical finding. First, I stopped at a local clinic. "Hello, I'm here for a pregnancy test." No one flinched. *How could they not be as nervous as I was?* I was impatiently waiting in the examination room when the nurse came back in and said, "You're pregnant."

"Just exactly *how* pregnant am I?"

She told me my HCG levels indicated I was about three weeks pregnant but that I should visit my OB/GYN for a detailed answer.

Following the appointment, my intuition told me to head to my holistic doctor, Dr. Stein. I walked into her office, told her I was pregnant, and that Anthony and I were recessive carriers of CDG1-A, a disease that could be fatal for the embryo. Then I flippantly explained that I might have to terminate the pregnancy. The way I saw it (and I have asked God for forgiveness a million times over) was that I couldn't, in good conscience, bring a child into the world knowing it would suffer in a hospital every day it was alive. I didn't want to love a baby that I might not be able to know.

I was so matter-of-fact that it surprised Dr. Stein, but she sternly replied, "Stop it right now. Stop speaking that way. Words, beliefs, and intentions are powerful. The baby is connected with you. Speak life to your baby." She sat across from me in her faith-filled office and confidently reminded me that words and thoughts make a huge impact. She advised me to be positive and to act as if we were going to meet a strong, healthy baby in nine months.

By the end of the day, I had confirmed my pregnancy, and I was now doing all I could to carry a healthy, vibrant baby. I ditched alcohol, made room in our kitchen cabinets for pounds of vitamins, and started learning all I could. During my evening walks, I listened to Dr. Oz's *YOU: Having a Baby* and soaked in as much as I could. Early in the book, the authors touched on epigenetics, and I found this topic fascinating.

The way I understood it, I was able to turn certain genes in the baby's DNA on and off based on my attitude, my health, and the way I conducted myself. This included the way I ate, what I believed, and even how I went about approaching the day.[9] Was I stressed or calm? Did I live with anxiety, or did I live in a peaceful state? All these factors contributed to the genetic makeup of our baby. Wonderful news! I could influence our baby's development.

I did not entirely understand the science, but I knew that positivity and a healthy lifestyle could move mountains, and so I tried. I made the distinct choice to consume wholesome foods and beverages and I kept my thoughts and behaviors in line.

YOU: Having a Baby noted that even *in utero*, the baby experiences the world the way I experience the world. So, if I experienced the world as scarce, the baby would have the same thought process. If I dealt with adversity by being stressed and anxious, then the baby would learn to deal with adversity by

The world is safe + abundant.

being stressed and anxious. Conversely, if I acted as if the world were safe and abundant, then the baby would adopt those same perspectives.

I had my fair share of anxieties and insecurities, and I knew I did not want the baby to adopt these attributes, so I made it a goal to strengthen my mental health. I surrounded myself with peaceful people and peaceful settings. Sometimes, this meant slowly pulling away from friends, and sometimes, it meant having candid discussions with them, detailing my preferences for conduct around me. I believed and acted as if all the changes I made had an impact on the baby's health, because they did.

Amen

It was only early December, but I felt behind. There was so much information to take in—so much knowledge yet to accumulate.

Conventional advice told us to keep the pregnancy a secret until we completed our first trimester. We were only five weeks along, and twelve weeks seemed like an eternity away. We decided we'd wait to hear the baby's heartbeat and then tell our nearest and dearest.

I made an appointment with my OB/GYN. As he was both my doctor and a friend, I was jumping to share the news. His examination confirmed that I was, in fact, pregnant. One can never hear too many confirmations! And with modern technology, we were able to see our little baby and hear its reassuring heartbeat. *We have a heartbeat! We have a viable baby!*

The nursing staff said we should only let our close family know, as we would want their support. They advised against telling too many people in case the pregnancy didn't hold; it is much easier to tell folks good news than to unwind it. Unwinding it would be emotionally stressful for us at best, and painful at worst. They advised, "A miscarriage is difficult enough to deal with, without having to explain it to people."

I knew that if something happened, I'd be crushed, but I thought, *I'm going to cross that bridge when I get there. Right now, I'm going all in.* I wanted everyone's well wishes and prayers. I wanted every ounce of good energy I could garner to be felt and sensed by the baby. We wanted this baby, and we knew the baby was viable and strong. We spoke life to our baby, and we wanted everyone else to do the same. Anthony and I rolled the dice and put our emotions on the line. And though we weren't able to go scuba diving or travel to the Galapagos, we were able to create life out of love, and that has been the greatest adventure for which I could ever ask.

After the holiday season and spreading the good news, we left our beloved city of Austin and moved to Houston. We had experienced Austin collectively for over thirty years, and we were excited about what Houston had to offer. We bid farewell to our hippie house in our hippie neighborhood in our hippie city. Our new Houston home had all the makings of a grown-up home, and the nester in me beamed. The house was a perfect place to grow our family.

Just Between Us

Just between us, my holistic doctor made a huge difference. I was afraid of the genetic testing results and of ALL the possibly terrible outcomes, so I shut down. The moment I found out I was pregnant, I expected the worst. Everything else in my life had gone so well for so long that I was anticipating the other shoe dropping.

Dr. Stein was a godsend. Her words were so encouraging and resolute that I paid absolute attention to them. In the same way I wanted assurance I was pregnant, I wanted someone to give me permission to be excited, to be positive, and to move forward in light. She gave me that permission, and I took it. On my way out of her office, she prescribed loads of vitamins, and on the bottom of the prescription sheet she wrote, "Speak life." That piece of paper lived on our refrigerator for months. Every time I opened it (which was *a lot*—I was preggo, after all), I reminded myself, "Speak life."

I lived in the positive. I acted as if my actions mattered and like I was going to be a mama to a healthy baby. My inclination was to couch my joy to protect my heart ("just in case"), but with every positive word and action, I stepped further out on the limb of faith.

A lot of us live dreading the phone call in the middle of the night, but that dread, anxiety, and worry only dulls our present moment. It doesn't *actually* make the phone call less terrible. Just between us, anxiety cannot live in the present; it needs trials from the past or fears borrowed from the future as oxygen. But in the present, anxiety dies because RIGHT NOW there is something—many things, in fact—for which to be grateful. *Amen*

You have the power to banish the anxiety, the dread, and the worry from your life. You don't need it. It's not good for you. You are better than all the dirty lies that anxiety and worry tell you. If you devote yourself to living in the present and to practicing gratitude, you will be able to handle *anything* that comes your way.

**Anxiety cannot live in the present;
it needs trials from the past or fears borrowed
from the future as oxygen.**

Hope for Navigating—The Power of Your Thoughts

Pastor Joel Osteen speaks of the power of words in his book, *I Am*. He says that whatever descriptive words you use to complete an *I Am . . .* statement will find you.[10] Our thoughts and words mold our futures, and we can use them to create our own positive and even dreamy self-fulfilling prophecy.

Positive thinking has an amazing physiological component to substantiate its influence. Neuroscientists have discovered that repetitive thoughts (both positive and negative) form neural pathways. The more we activate and reinforce a particular thought or belief, the stronger those neural pathways become, and the more automatically they become our "go-to" pattern of perceiving. It's called *neuroplasticity*. Our brains have the innate ability to change our synaptic wiring. This means we have the opportunity to form new neural pathways, change our thinking, and ultimately, change our experiences.[11]

An old Chinese proverb captures the power of our thinking in shaping our lives:

> Sow a thought and reap an act;
> Sow an act and reap a habit;
> Sow a habit and reap a character;
> Sow a character and reap a destiny.

Belief is a powerful tool in creating the life you want, but it takes impartial self-reflection—and a dedication to act on what you believe—to wield it effectively. When confronted with the many possibilities that a pregnancy posed, especially with our genetic testing results, I chose to do everything in my power to live in the positive and act daily in a way that reflected that assurance. I was stalwart in giving my baby the best possible environment to grow and thrive, free of anxiety and fear.

The Law of Attraction—the idea that "like attracts like"—espouses that we are responsible for bringing both positive and negative influences into our lives, whether we realize it or not. A key part of this ideology is understanding that *where we place our focus* has an intense impact on what happens to us.[12] For example, if we spend our days wallowing in regrets about the past or anxiety about our future, we'll likely see more negativity appearing. On the other hand, if we look for the silver lining, the beauty, the divine in every experience, we'll soon start to see positivity surrounding us every day.

When we choose to notice and nurture the positive around us, we are choosing to transform our lives. Let's focus on the positive and watch it compound.

"Create the highest, grandest vision for your life. Then let every step move you in that direction. You become what you believe."
—Oprah Winfrey

I am safe.
I am abundant.
I am present.
I am enough.

Trail Journal

What are some negative thoughts that you let yourself believe?

People aren't trustworthy.

Can you replace those thoughts with positive ones?

YES *The world is a generous place!*

Is there a current situation in which you need to "speak life"?

Chapter 9

TESTING THE BABY

There was a 25 percent chance the baby would inherit both our recessive genes, and I wanted to learn all I could about the situation. I knew the testing would be more involved than a regular checkup, so I started the process right away. *Who would I call? Who would I see? What would they say?*

The phone trail was long and tedious. I started off by speaking with our original fertility clinic in San Antonio. They sent our blood test results to Baylor University Medical Center. After a doctor at Baylor analyzed and confirmed the results, they referred me to a genetic counseling service. The service helped us wade through all our possible paths. Then the doctor at Baylor advised me to make an appointment in Houston with a specialist, one of only three doctors in the state of Texas who could perform the next procedure we needed, Chorionic Villus Sampling (CVS), a diagnostic test for identifying chromosomal abnormalities and other inherited disorders. Between the initial phone calls and the wait time and the "we'll get back to you," messages, the process took weeks.

The eight weeks or so between discovering we were pregnant and the CVS test date were excruciatingly nerve-racking. *Was the baby healthy? Would the baby survive?* I tried to stay in the light, but in the back of my mind, I knew there was a possibility we would not have a fairytale ending. By January 27, I had been carrying the baby for almost three months! I had heard its heartbeat and seen its head, its tiny arms, and its tiny legs. I was connected to the baby, and yet there was a chance the baby wouldn't survive. It was a heavy weight.

Before we went into the CVS examination room, Anthony and I were led into a meeting room with our genetic counselor, Rebecca. We sat and watched as she pulled out a thick three-ring binder filled with diagrams and detailed medical information. She described the results of our blood tests from the fertility clinic in San Antonio. But since I had already spoken with doctors and genetic counselors and done independent research, I knew most of what she was telling us. After about ten minutes of basic explanation, we told her we had done our homework and that she could skip ahead.

She proceeded to go into great detail about what would happen if the baby had both of our recessive CDG1-A genes. Using hand-drawn diagrams, Rebecca showed us the four possible DNA combinations for this one gene, and then she talked about the worst-case scenario. But *our* minds were not focused on the worst-case scenario, and we didn't want hers to be either. Anthony politely asked her to skip over the "what happens if" part and move on. Rebecca, not really understanding what we wanted, continued talking about what would happen if we received the worst possible news.

We sat at a circular beige table, the fluorescent lights shining overhead. Anthony held my left hand in his and sternly told Rebecca that he understood it was part of her job to explain the possibilities, but that he didn't want to hear it. He informed her that continuing the discussion was giving me anxiety and that he saw no reason for it. He thanked her and told her we'd cross the worst-case scenario bridge when we got there. Until then, we were praying for the best.

We walked into the examination room and Dr. Smith, one of the three doctors in Texas who performed CVS testing, met us. I undressed from the waist down, as I had grown accustomed to doing, and waited for him to start the procedure. The doctor put me at ease and inserted the catheter.

It wasn't excruciating, but there was definitely pain involved. Using the catheter, Dr. Smith removed some chorionic villus cells from my placenta, at the point where it attached to the uterine wall. I held my husband's hand for support as tiny tears rolled down the outside of my cheeks. I wanted to both *appear* calm and brave and *BE* calm and brave. Dr. Smith *Right* finished the procedure and assured us the results were going to indicate a healthy baby. In such a heavy moment, his words of reassurance lifted my spirit.

In the days that followed, I went to God. I knew that whatever I was going through was for my own good. I knew that there was a lesson to be learned, and the process would eventually strengthen me. But even though I knew it would all work out the way *God* wanted, *I* wanted it to work out the way *I* wanted. I wanted a healthy baby. I wanted God to want me to have a healthy baby. And no matter how much I wanted it, I knew I could not control the outcome. So I prayed and prayed and prayed.

And then in all my emotion, I surrendered the outcome to God.

One night, Anthony and I were lying on our mattress, which was still on the floor as we hadn't finished moving in yet. With our dogs, Beau Jackson and Mischa, near, we settled in for the night. With them so close, we were able to love on them, and in such a worrisome time, their presence brought me peace. They lay right beside us, and we stroked their backs and rubbed their bellies. The love in the room was palpable. It was a special time for the four of us.

Once we all had one last go at the bathroom, we turned on our nightlights, and I nuzzled into my husband. Our warm skin touching, I told him that I surrendered the outcome to God. I told him that I was scared but that we would be okay if faced with the worst-case scenario. "If this pregnancy is not meant to be, then there's a lesson in that. We will learn from this, survive it, and be okay." My words were big, and I didn't totally embody them, but I knew I needed to. We shared our fears, felt each other's heartbeats, and gave it to God. "Be still and know that I am God," Psalm 46:10.

Exactly ten days after the CVS, I called our genetic counselor to check on test results, but they weren't ready. The cell development had to be observed for a minimum of ten days, but it would most likely take fourteen days. Though I had surrendered, my thoughts still swirled. *Would the baby be healthy?*

Two days later, I was headed to our local pharmacy when Rebecca called. She told me the lab needed a few more days to be 100 percent certain of their results, but the results as they stood were 90 percent certain. Then she asked me if I would like to know the findings anyway. Her question was so quick I didn't even have time to hope, or to think, but I did have time to feel. And in my heart, I felt calm. "Go ahead."

"The baby is not a carrier of the gene at all."

"What?!"

Just like there was a 25 percent chance the baby would adopt both recessive genes, there was a 25 percent chance the baby would not adopt the gene at all. The baby was 100 percent healthy and did not carry the CDG1-A gene at all! She continued to say that all signs pointed to a healthy baby girl. *A healthy baby girl!*

I turned around and headed home to tell Anthony. The pharmacy could wait. I walked through the front door and up the stairs to Anthony's office. I opened the door, and the words came rushing out. "Rebecca called with news. She said the baby is 100 percent fine! The baby is healthy. The baby shows no signs of CDG1-A! They aren't 100 percent ready to make the call—they need a few more days to be certain—but they are pretty confident. Our baby is healthy!"

The weight had been lifted, and a little lady was on her way to us.

Just Between Us

When our genetic counselor called with good news, I was thrilled and deeply grateful. Our baby was 100 percent healthy. We, in fact, did not have to cross the worst-case scenario bridge! We were bestowed with the best-case scenario!

Just between us, my surrender to God was HUGE. When I surrendered, my mindset was an enormous leap from where I had begun when Anthony and I started dating. Remember that when I met Anthony I thought that being able to give him a child was a reason for him to love me more? For me to get to a place where I could say, "We will survive this heartbreak," I *also* had to fully resolve in my heart that Anthony really did love me for *me*—that he, in fact, had married me for my company and my gifts and not my *potential* gifts. It was also tremendous in that I had surrendered to God's will. ALL my sanity was on the line, and I gave it to God. Whatever the outcome, whatever the timing, it would all be good. Somehow, I would be blessed, even though I didn't see how. And just between us—the same goes for your life. *amen*

I thanked God for his mercy and for trusting me with the life of this child. I felt privileged; not every woman is afforded the opportunity to bear children, and some put years of effort into conceiving. Sometimes it works, and sometimes it doesn't. But for some reason, this gift had been bestowed upon me. And keeping in mind all the heartache of women who try but don't successfully conceive, I treated my pregnancy with the utmost respect.

Whatever the outcome, whatever the timing, it would all be good. Somehow, I would be blessed, even though I didn't see how. And just between us—the same goes for your life.

Hope for Navigating—Surrender

Surrender acknowledges that, ultimately, we don't have control over certain circumstances. It's graciously handing over the outcome to someone else, and then making the most of that outcome. (I'm not sure there's even another way, but there is certainly the illusion of it.) And the more life I live, the more I realize that life is balancing the tension between trying our best and honoring the situations God puts us in.

When I sincerely surrendered the fate of our baby to God, I was saying "I trust you, whatever that outcome may be." We may be able to see what's around the corner, but God is able to see our *entire* life's path. And circumstance by circumstance, he is gently guiding us along in a way that we might be able to have the greatest connection and loving impact with those around us.

Few have modeled surrender more faithfully and completely than Mother Teresa. Giving her life in wholehearted dedication to the poorest of the poor, her example is one that stirs the soul. In a collection of her words entitled *Total Surrender*, Mother Teresa tells of the simple joy of following Jesus and surrendering fully to him. She says, "Total surrender to God must come in small details just as it comes in big details. It's nothing but that single word—yes. I accept whatever you give, and I give whatever you take."

When I sincerely surrendered the fate of our baby to God, I was saying "I trust you, whatever that outcome may be."

Surrender can be gut-wrenching. When all we want to do it make sure that it all turns out okay, or that it all turns out the "right" way, or the way we would like, surrender can seem inconceivable. Each of us walks a different path, and some of us never quite experience surrender, and that's okay. We will know when to surrender because we have done every single thing in our power to create a good outcome, we have reached and stretched in ways we never thought possible, and we have hit *the wall*. And while I don't think surrender is always necessary, I do think that when surrender occurs, a peace settles our spirits. Once we have tried our best and surrendered the outcome, we are saying, "I know it may not feel good, and I may not like it, but somehow, someway, this is for my benefit, and I will be okay."

> *"But now, O LORD, you are our Father, we are the clay,*
> *and you our potter; and all of us are the work of*
> *your hand," Isaiah 64:8*

Trail Journal

Is there something you have been longing for?

Would you consider praying about it?

Would you consider that what you have been longing for may come to you in a different form or at a different time?

Chapter 10

PAIN

One day, as I was organizing my bedroom closet, I started to feel some real pain by my right hip bone. I knew of round ligament pain, but I wasn't sure whether this was what I was experiencing. Wanting to self-diagnose and save myself a trip to the doctor's office, I Googled, Web MD'd, and searched mommy blogs. They all described the pain I was having and advised taking warm baths, resting with a pillow between my legs, and practicing aromatherapy. I tried the suggestions but found no relief. In fact, as the hours went by, the pain worsened.

In a panic, I called my OB/GYN in McAllen and explained my symptoms. He also thought my symptoms sounded like round ligament pain. There was nothing more he suggested I do, but he did tell me that as the pregnancy progressed, the pain would get worse. *If that was round ligament pain and it would get much worse, what was my labor going to feel like? Would I be able to handle it?* I continued trying all the suggested remedies, and yet, hour by hour, the pain mounted.

It was unquestionably the worst pain I had ever felt. It hurt to stand upright, to walk, and even to shower. I dreaded every trip to the bathroom. I'd grip through the pain and pray: "Jesus, please help me pee; please help me get through this." I had to pray to pee! I had no idea what was going on, but it was terrifying. *Was the baby okay? Was I okay? Was this normal? We had escaped a bad result with the genetic testing. Was this the moment I had been dreading all along?*

As far as I knew, my round ligament was stretching and nothing could be done about it, so I went about my daily activities. And a few days into the pain, I figured out that if I bent forward from the hips—with my back parallel to the floor—and walked slowly, I could get around without too much issue. Obstinate.

One afternoon, hunched over, I pulled a chair in front of the stove and sat while I sizzled pork chops in a pan. But soon, smoke filled the kitchen. Anthony was on a work call upstairs, and I didn't want the smoke alarms to go off, so I tried to open a window. Bent over, not engaging my core, I pulled the chair as close to the counter as possible, braced myself on the back of the chair, reached over the counter and the kitchen sink to the bottom of the window sill, and tried to push it up. Nothing. I had no muscle control. I could not even push a window up! *I was a Tough Mudder, a marathon runner, a Crossfitter ... and I couldn't push up a window! Preposterous.* I felt defeated.

As the kitchen filled with smoke, I sat in the chair, sobbing, when out of nowhere a thought popped into my head—or maybe God put it there. I thought about the millions of women who would trade spots with me in a New York minute. They would gladly trade a few weeks of pain for the blessing of bringing a life into the world; they wouldn't hesitate. Perspective. And although my pain remained, I managed and complained less.

A few weeks into the pain, I was slated to attend a work event. *How would I manage?* I was to fly to McAllen, work the event, and fly back. I wanted to go, so I prepared for the weekend trip. I had no idea how long the pain would rage, but if it was going to stick around and possibly get worse, I was going to have to find a way to live with it and go about my business. I packed a suitcase and cried the entire twenty-minute drive to the airport. The slightest movement induced pain. Even breathing too deeply caused aching. Anthony asked me repeatedly if I was sure I wanted to go. I told him that I was and kissed him goodbye.

Somehow, I managed to work through the pain that weekend, but I finally surrendered. I made a doctor's appointment; I needed answers. My mom and I walked through the normally busy medical facility to my doctor's office and were sweetly shown into the examination room. My OB/GYN started the sonogram machine and waited patiently for it to warm up. He smothered the wand with gel and proceeded to rub it all over my exposed belly. "There's your baby," he said.

"She's okay?"

"She's fine."

The words fell so sweetly on my spirit. "Can I hear her heartbeat?"

"Sure you can." He found the sound of her heartbeat and turned up the volume. It sounded like a timpani drum—significant, and yet round and billowy. Her heartbeat was strong, she was swimming around, and I felt relief.

He continued to explore around my belly. "There's your problem. You have a tomato-sized fibroid." He explained that a fibroid was a muscular tumor, and it was growing on the wall of my uterus. He told me it was benign, but that I'd have to learn to manage the pain as it could not be treated during the pregnancy.

"So I'm going to live with this pain for four more months?" The word "months" took me twice as long as usual to say.

"Yes," the doctor replied. "We can hope that the fibroid turns on itself and decreases in size due to lack of blood supply, but beyond that, it's only pain management."

Even though the pain was still there, I felt a huge relief knowing where the pain was coming from and that our baby girl was safe.

I flew back to Houston, and when Anthony picked me up from the airport, the air was thick and wet, and it looked like it was just about to rain. In Houston, it was *always* just about to rain. But on this day in late March, the air was particularly humid, and I looked over at my husband trying to grip the steering wheel. The humidity level was sending his arthritis through the roof. His joints hurt so bad that he couldn't completely wrap his fingers around the wheel; he was maneuvering with his palms. We knew that the increase in humidity from Austin to Houston was going to be a factor for his arthritis—just not *how much* of a factor.

We had been in Houston sixty days, and we had spent a good chunk of change moving between cities and settling into our new home. I had established care with a doctor who would deliver our baby, found a neighborhood grocery store, and settled into a routine. We were finally comfortable in Houston, and yet ... he wasn't. As I looked over at him trying to grip the steering wheel, I knew we had to leave Houston. No amount of settling in was worth having my husband uncomfortable. So on the drive home from the airport, I said, "I think we should move back to Austin. This weather is terrible, and we need to get you to a better place." We sat on it for a couple of days, and by mid-week, I had reserved a moving company. We gave ourselves six weeks to wrap up our affairs in Houston; we planned to be living back in Austin by mid-May.

Just Between Us

The fibroids were intensely painful. I was scared that something was wrong with the baby, and I was equally scared of the scathing pain. But after the thought popped into my head about all the women who are unable to conceive, my attitude shifted. I felt as if remaining grateful through the pain was an opportunity to communicate to God that he could trust me to honor and praise him, no matter the situation. It was almost a moment of transcendence: I changed my environment based on how I perceived it. Additionally, it was an opportunity to honor a good friend who had been unable to conceive. Every time I felt like complaining, I'd think about her and her years of heartache. I carried my baby for my husband and me and, in part, for my girlfriend.

When we began preparing for the move back to Austin, I was busy calling movers, calling different medical practices, cancelling subscriptions, rerouting mail, cancelling the cable, calling the gas company—the list seemed to go on and on. *Where would we live? What doctor would I see? Would a doctor even take me so late in the pregnancy? Would the nursery be ready in time? We were twelve weeks away; what if she came early?* I knew we needed to move, and in no way did I want to prolong my husband's discomfort, but I didn't actually *want* to tear down and pack up one house *and* set up and settle into an entirely different, unfamiliar house. So after a few weeks of what seemed like constant motion, I freaked out. I was overwhelmed by the reality of setting up shop—*again*—at twenty-eight weeks pregnant!

We didn't have any baby gear; there was no nursery and no doctor! *What would we do if she showed up early?* This was the third time we had packed boxes in six months, and I was at the end of my rapidly fraying rope. My husband held my hand, apologized for all the chaos, and offered a host of solutions. In the end, his compassion was enough to keep me afloat. Compassion is wonderful that way.

**It was almost a moment of transcendence:
I changed my environment based on how
I perceived it.**

I was in pain, and so was my husband. We each needed tending, and we did our best to make sure we gave each other what we needed. And just between us, I freaked out a little, but I could have freaked out a lot. There was A LOT going on.

Hope for Navigating—The Transformative Power of Pain

Pain can show up in our lives physically as well as emotionally. Sometimes it knocks on our doors both ways simultaneously, and it's never enjoyable, but it always leaves a fresh perspective. *yes it really does not hurt*

Suffering can cause a slew of questions to come bubbling to the surface. *How did I get here? Could I have done anything different? Why is this happening to me? How can I stop this? How can I move forward? How can I heal? What else do I need? What is going on?!* Discomfort, whether it's a throbbing ankle or a throbbing heart, makes us so acutely aware of its presence that it's difficult to focus on anything else.

While I was experiencing physical pain, I felt frustrated, crippled, and even angry. *WHY?!* But when the thought popped into my head about remaining grateful, it made the experience less traumatic.

When we experience pain, we have a choice to allow it to teach us something valuable, as it often will, or to ultimately derail us. I could have justifiably wallowed in my pain. Yet I made a conscious decision to allow gratitude to transform the experience, shifting my focus from physical pain to gratitude, eventually changing me for the better.

In Glennon Doyle Melton's book, *Carry On Warrior*, she writes,

> "Pain is not a sign that you've taken a wrong turn or that you're doing life wrong. It's not a signal that you need a different life or partner or body or home or personality. Pain is not a hot potato to pass on to the next person or generation. Pain is not a mistake to fix. Pain is just a sign that a lesson is coming. Discomfort is purposeful: it is there to teach you what you need to know so you can become who you were meant to be. Pain is just a traveling professor. When pain knocks on the door, wise

ones breathe deep and say: 'Come in. Sit down with me. And don't leave until you've taught me what I need to know.'"[3] *Yeah. Lord, what do I need to learn from this pain? 3/28/18*

When faced with pain, we can allow ourselves to be overrun with resentment or bitterness, or we can go deep into ourselves and allow moments of pain to reveal truths to us. It is through pain that we have the opportunity to become more closely acquainted with humility, compassion, and—most importantly—the life-giving quality of empathy.

When we experience pain, we have a choice to allow it to teach us something valuable, as if often will, or to ultimately derail us.

"God will not look you over for medals, degrees, or diplomas, but for scars."
–Elbert Hubbard

Come on with this.

Trail Journal

What is your usual reaction to pain?

Bitterness
Rage
very reactive at times

How do you think you will approach pain now, after reading this chapter?

After the Lord
heals —
gentler,
Humbler.

Have there been moments of pain in your life that have transformed you?

Yes.

Chapter 11

THE SEX PROBLEM

I was ill-equipped for the body changes that came with pregnancy. I just wasn't ready to give my body away. But with every passing day, my boobs got bigger, my *linea negra* (the line of hair from just below my bra line to my pubic bone) got darker, and my thighs got plumper. My morphing created some *serious* stress in my life. I did not want to look PREGNANT, just cute and pregnant, you know—like in the magazines. For me to feel beautiful, I needed to be magazine-cover worthy, photo-ready. And since I didn't think I was either, I became obsessed with my changing body. My ego and my vanity did not allow for the fact that I was creating and carrying a human life.

Layered on top of my body issues was the fact that sex had evaded our relationship for weeks and weeks. *When would we? Would we ever? What was going on?* We had gone long enough that it had become awkward. Wash face, brush teeth, read a book, go to bed. Night after night after night. *Where had our sex life gone?* I wanted to broach the subject, but I didn't want to risk getting hurt. Just because you're married doesn't mean you won't be vulnerable, remember? *What had happened to us? Was I inadequate?*

I wanted sex and wanted to feel sexual with my husband. After all, my sex drive needed attention. But in front of Anthony, I became reserved and self-conscious. I was barely far enough along in my own sexual revolution to feel confident pre-pregnancy, so the idea of being confident in the bedroom *while* pregnant—FORGET ABOUT IT. Being pregnant and feeling confident in the bedroom is like being in an alternate universe. It's *completely* different. And even though I had read that not all men were into sex with pregnant women, and even though I was warned not to take it personally, I felt rejected.

One night, we began kissing, and in the way a woman can tell, I knew sex was around the corner. I began to get nervous, and my palms began to sweat. *Was it actually happening?* There were three of us in the bedroom: Anthony, me, and our growing baby. I didn't want to bring attention to my belly, and so I asked him to turn off the lights—as if dim lighting would make a basketball disappear. He did, and we continued kissing gently. But after several minutes, Anthony stopped. "I can't do this. The pregnancy is freaking me out. The notion of a baby being inside you ... I can't."

His words shot to my heart, and my spirit broke into a million pieces. I was devastated. Not having sex—and not talking about not having sex—was rough, but not having sex and knowing that my body had something to do with it was considerably worse.

What was I supposed to do? Leave the room? Stay? Cry? I was mortified!

I stayed on my side of the bed, as I didn't want to be touched, and silently sobbed. And even though he prodded me to say something—anything—I just couldn't. I wanted to be alone, so I walked a few feet to our bathroom, shut the door, and sobbed uncontrollably. I was wailing on the cold marble floor, and I didn't want to be seen. He asked multiple times for me to come back to bed, and even though I didn't want to oblige, I finally did.

He apologized profusely and said he knew how much something like this hurt me. He continued by saying he wanted to be honest and that we needed to talk about IT.

Hearing the honest reason—that the baby I was growing inside of me freaked him out—wounded me deeply. Hormones. On my best days, my low self-esteem hovered, and on my worst days, it walked with me hand-in-hand. I was pregnant, my body was unrecognizable, and my hormones dominated.

I was especially frustrated because I couldn't do anything about my growing belly. It wasn't going anywhere and, in fact, was getting bigger by the day! Before pregnancy, when my ego felt threatened, I would subdue it by exercising, eating less, or shopping—anything to make me feel more attractive. But I was pregnant, and I had handcuffed myself to the well-being of the baby. "I can't do anything about the way I look or feel!" I declared angrily. I felt shitty, and I wanted him to know it.

Negative thoughts flew through my mind, and I didn't want to be near my husband. I wanted to be distracted, so I left the bedroom, plopped down on the living room couch, and began binge-watching television. Television was the only vice I had left. All the vices that I previously tapped into were unavailable. I couldn't drink, I couldn't stay out late, and I couldn't really even binge eat because I was afraid of what binge eating would do to the baby. It was late, I didn't have anyone to call, and I wasn't even sure I wanted to call anyone. I wasn't ready to admit that my husband didn't want to have sex with me. *yeah.*

Intellectually, I knew he did not find me unattractive. All the baby books and blogs I read warned that most pregnant couples have a drop-off in sex, but I was sure it wouldn't happen to us. Deep down, I knew it wasn't me, but it *felt* like me, and that feeling caused a great deal of pain. I was hurt and outraged. *How could he possibly say those things to me?*

I curled up on the couch and watched episode after episode of *The West Wing*. I was worn from our attempted sex debacle and faded in and out of sleep, yet I refused to go back to bed. I was intent on staying on the couch to show Anthony just how bad I felt, just how much he had hurt my feelings. Passive aggressive award! *hahahahaha*

But at around three or four o'clock in the morning, Anthony walked from the bedroom to the living room and peeled me off the couch. My eyes barely open, I saw him walking toward me. I exhaled in relief. I didn't put up one ounce of resistance. Anthony's noticing I wasn't in bed made me feel valued and consoled. The moment I saw him, my anger softened. *He still wanted me to sleep next to him.* He held me as we walked into the bedroom, and even though my feelings were still hurt, I melted into him like a pat of butter on a hot piece of toast. I wanted to be close to him. We wouldn't have sex, but we would be with each other.

The next day, even though I didn't think it would, the sun crept up the horizon, the morning newspapers were delivered, and the coffee was brewed. I woke up wounded and searched myself for courage. *How would I be able to face my husband in the light of day?* I brushed my teeth and stalled before heading into the kitchen for breakfast. I dreaded facing Anthony and the embarrassment that would accompany it. *What would I say? How would I react? Would we address last night?* I took an extra fifteen minutes to pull myself together. I walked out of our bedroom and straight into my safe place—his lap. I curled into his chest and wept. "I'm so sorry, I don't know what to do, and I'm embarrassed. This is embarrassing for me. You are not attracted to me, and yet there's nothing I can do to fix the situation. In fact, I'm getting bigger and more unattractive by the day." His words the night before had seared into the most fragile parts of my self-esteem.

He assured me that I had no reason to be embarrassed, and he apologized for hurting me so deeply. He said he knew his honesty hit all my insecurities, but that honesty was our best chance at weathering the storm. He didn't understand my embarrassment, but he said we would work through it. And then he suggested something that changed the fabric of our marriage: "We should not sleep separately. When we are the maddest or the most hurt, when we want time or distance from each other, that's when we've GOT to stay in the same bed. Separating creates literal and figurative distance at an already fractured time." He was right, and as each day passed, my anxiety around the situation lessened.

Soon, days turned into weeks and weeks turned into a month, but we were no closer to getting it on. Most days, I found a sense of calm about the issue, but there were other days when it was really tough. I missed sex, but infinitely more important, I missed connecting through intimacy. It's often said that men need sex to connect, and women need to connect to have sex. I was smack dab in the middle, needing both equally and simultaneously. For weeks, Anthony praised my patience, but it was wearing thin as there was no resolution in sight. I wanted a solution, and I knew my ever-growing belly wasn't helping the situation. Finally, on the night before Easter, my heavy thoughts and impatience took over.

Driven by my compounding anxiety, I started to devise ways to be passive aggressive. My thoughts swirled and led me down dark alleys, leaving sanity behind. *What was happening? Was my marriage okay? How would this turn out? How were we going to resolve this?* I was a mess and prayed to my Grandma Oralia. (She went to be with the Lord in 2006, and yet I feel her presence now more than ever.) I asked her for strength, grace, and peace of mind.

My prayers were answered, as somewhere in my scheming I came back to my right mind—I knew I needed to ask for help. So, after tossing and turning all night, I walked out into the living room on Easter morning, and, with sleep in my eyes and a lump in my throat, I sat on Anthony's lap. "I need help. I need professional help. My anxiety is too much, and I don't have a solution. I need help."

I didn't know what else to do. I had read, prayed, worked out, and distracted myself. Nothing worked. I needed professional help. And after I admitted it, my anxiety seemed less daunting, and I felt stronger and at ease. I kissed him, went into the kitchen to pour myself some coffee, and found, sitting in a corner of the room, this *ENORMOUS* flower arrangement. The arrangement was made up of spectacular red roses and calla lilies. And there was a hand-written note from Anthony.

I wept. I wasn't sure what the occasion was. *Did he think I needed a pick-me-up? Was he trying to be romantic?* In the end, the *why* wasn't important. What was important was that it was exceptionally thoughtful, and I was incredibly grateful. Moreover, the arrangement was conspicuously perfect because of the lilies. My Grandma Oralia was a florist, and she often used lilies in her creations, so they evoked her memory.

While I prayed to her that morning, she was in the house. She was with me the entire time, and God was with me the entire time.

Later that afternoon, while I was dressing, I felt a little something in my belly. I felt definite movement. I held my breath and waited to feel it again. *Again! There it is again!* "Honey, honey, come here!" I called. "I'm not sure if you'll be able to feel it, but the baby is kicking!" I lay on my back and placed his hand on the spot just where I thought the baby would kick next. We eagerly waited and after a few seconds, there she was!

"Did you move?" he asked me.

"Nope! That wasn't me! That was the baby!"

"What?!"

We stayed there for a few minutes, waiting and feeling. Our healthy baby was moving around, and we felt her; it was divine. Anthony tenderly explained to her how loved and safe she was. And he let her know that she could take her time and that there was no rush.

I didn't seek professional therapy right away, but Anthony and I continued talking about our lack of intimacy. Talking made the situation less intimidating, and it seemed like maybe one day we would overcome it. In the days following, we made concerted efforts to connect by being extra tender and sweet with each other. Our relationship did not need sex, but it *did* need connection.

Just Between Us

Just between us, my body image issues were not a product of my pregnancy. I had them *before* I was pregnant, so carrying a baby—with the extra pounds and physical changes that result—weighed (literally!) on my already fragile self-esteem. I had a difficult time keeping perspective. I viewed it as my *belly*, not as the *baby*. I was focused on how much weight I was gaining and overlooked the fact that my body was a vessel for a growing *human being*. I wanted to look like a movie star and thought that only when I looked like one was I worthy. It was total insanity, but it was my reality. I never viewed other women as "less than," but my ego was so large and in charge that I held myself to a different standard. Talk about missing the forest for the trees. Focusing on the three-pound weight gain rather than the fact that my body was *creating* another human being was troubling. My low self-esteem, coupled with a pause in our sex life, made for excellent times! My anxiety ran amuck!

As far as I can tell, sex lives come in all shapes and sizes, and that's no different for couples who are pregnant. Sex with a pregnant woman is loaded. I was transforming, and I also spent all day, every day, looking at my ever-changing body. My darker skin, my hairier arms, my curvier hips ... I had time to get to know it and familiarize myself. Anthony did not. One day, he had a wife who fit into her jeans, and the next, he had a wife with water balloons for boobs and a basketball for a belly. Boom, pow, pregnant! I was so caught up in my hormones that I didn't give my husband any space to adjust. I wanted him to treat me like the vixen I clearly was!

Just between us, I was also wrapped up in fear that our sex life would never return, that our marriage would be forever changed. I feared he would never again view me as hot, but *only* as a mom.

But in the way that only God does, he provided. Easter morning, we celebrated Jesus's resurrection, and we also celebrated the making new of our marriage. The night before, Anthony and I had dealt with some real emotions and experienced each other in such honest ways that our marriage and family were forever fortified by it.

On the day we moved from Houston back to Austin, I finally reached out for professional help; I'd be damned if my baby inherited my anxiety. I wanted to give her every possible chance to go through life peaceful and kind. My goal was for her to feel special, valued, loved, and complete from the inside out. I knew that even in our baby's infancy, she would observe my actions and thought processes, and so I was extra motivated to clean up my act.

Just as I had done the sugar cleanse the previous July, I wanted to do a mental cleanse so that our baby would be as healthy as possible. I wanted to be in the best frame of mind—as a woman, a wife, and a mama.

Hope for Navigating—Sex and Your Self-Esteem

I struggled with body image issues for the better part of two decades, and so it was no surprise that they plagued me in the bedroom during pregnancy. Sex during pregnancy, with all the physical contortions it would involve with my growing belly, paled in comparison to the mental contortions I practiced.

As our sexual dry spell dragged on without an end in sight, I felt like a batter coming up to the plate in constant fear of striking out. It got to the point where I didn't even want to risk an at-bat. It took me some time to pinpoint it, but for me, it wasn't about the actual sex: it was about wanting to be wanted. *yeah. Of course, we all feel this!*

Dr. Laura Berman, sex expert, says, "Low self-worth can definitely throw a wrench into your love life—and into your bedroom. After all, how can you really let go and enjoy sexual pleasure if you feel ashamed or unhappy in your own skin?"[14] Dr. Berman gives us hope when she outlines ways we can improve our self-esteem, thereby improving our sex life in the process. She suggests getting to the root of low self-worth and continues by emphasizing that partners aren't responsible for our moods or our self-esteems—only *we* are in charge of our emotional health.

Sex can be complicated. There are layers and layers of assumptions, insecurities, desires, secret desires, and expectations. I dare not generalize the physical or emotional nature of the meeting of two souls. Instead, let's encourage each other to *talk about it*. Whether we're talking about it with our girlfriends, our therapists, or our partners, let's keep talking. Let's keep trying to put words to how we feel and what we want, and eventually, we will find a place where we can be comfortable.

It took me some time to pinpoint it, but for me, it wasn't about the actual sex: it was about wanting to be wanted.

"Intimacy is the fiber that binds us to the people we love, and is built on time, investment, and honest communication. In a healthy long-term relationship, intimacy increases with time, and many men and women are fortunate to have a lover who is also their best friend. Sex and romance are crucial for long-term intimacy. The stronger the sexual connection, the stronger the emotional intimacy will be. It is important to nurture and feed your relationship both emotionally and sexually."

–Dr. Laura Berman

Trail Journal

Do you sometimes feel like you get in your own way when it comes to enjoying sex?

Do you view sex as physical or both physical and emotional?

Does sex have a positive, negative or neutral effect on your self-esteem?

Chapter 12

LIFE CAN BE JOYFUL

It was early May, and my cousin and I headed to a beach town for a friend's wedding. We were only there for one night, but it was enough time to get out of my own head. I was elated to have a sparkly dress in my closet that fit and to have such a fun date. Getting a little sun and feeling the ocean breeze would be a wonderful mood booster.

I was friends with both the bride and groom, and I wanted to support them, but I just knew I'd be back in the hotel by eight o'clock. After all, I was *really* pregnant!

We arrived at the church for the ceremony, and as we gathered our things, I saw three of my good friends from my days at The University of Texas, known as the Forty Acres. They were groomsmen! During our years on the Forty Acres, the four of us had hung out, studied, and gone out on the town together. In 2001, as entering freshman, we clung to each other, partly because we were Mexican and all from small towns, and partly because we were hard workers. But as often happens, once we graduated from UT, we drifted apart. Now my friends were all together for the wedding, *and* they would be there for the reception, *and* it was going to be so much fun! All of a sudden, I was ready to stay out *way* past eight! I'd stay out until nine, maybe even *ten*! Sound the alarms. I had not planned on having a great time, but it looked like I was going to after all.

That night, God granted me lightheartedness. I was so full of joy and had a night's reprieve from worrying about the pregnancy, the move, and my ever-changing body. My friends and I salsa-danced together, laughed, caught up, took photos, and enjoyed one another's families. My heart was deeply satisfied. It was fantastic to sit back and enjoy the fruits of our labor. All our hard work had paid off.

That weekend, I confided in my cousin about my sex life. I wanted to vent. I explained to her how nervous I was to approach the subject with Anthony. If I tried and Anthony and I couldn't go through with it, then I would be that much more devastated. She offered some suggestions, and right away, I thought: *You're not in my position. You have no idea!* Hormones. I realized I was more nervous about initiating sex with my husband than I was about willingly jumping out of a plane from ten thousand feet in the air. It was absurd!

When I returned to Houston, I communicated my nervousness to Anthony. I told him I wanted to get naked with him, but I was scared; the stakes were high. He agreed. I even admitted to being *less* afraid of jumping out of an airplane than approaching sex. He had a good laugh, and then we both decided to give it a go, but the pending move from Houston to Austin gave us ample time to make excuses and postpone.

Just Between Us

The weekend of my friends' wedding, I broke a cultural and societal mold. I grew up in a culture where wives *do not* go to weddings on their own, and they certainly don't dance with friends of the opposite sex, *with* or *without* their husbands present. And since that's what I learned as a young girl growing up on the Texas/Mexico border, I had always held myself to those cultural standards. But Anthony was different; he sincerely wanted me to enjoy myself. He was enthusiastic about my joy! The day after the wedding, I told him how much I danced and how much I enjoyed myself—and he was happy for me! It was a wonderful sensation to share joy with him and be met with gladness. I could spread my wings and enjoy life without fear of offending my husband.

Just between us, you don't have to do it the way you have always seen it done. It's okay to question the patterns with which you have been raised. Why do you do the things that you do? Do they make you happy? Do they create stress? Why not create a new normal, one that works for both people in your relationship? *yes, yes, yes*

Later that month, when we were settling into our new Austin home, I was frustrated because my belly was getting in the way. The heat and humidity made every task annoying. There was always a sheen of sweat at the nape of my neck. I needed a release and knew sex would help. I couldn't exactly seduce Anthony, though, bloated and all. But after garnering enough good sleep and courage, I proposed sex, out loud. "Let's just give it a go!" I walked into our bedroom, guarded, ready for the worst, ready for us to stop in the middle, ready to have it not quite work out. *What would happen? My belly was bigger than ever. How would he react? Would I be laughable? How could I possibly look sexy? Feel sexy? Was I crazy for even trying?* Turns out, it all turned out! We made love, big belly and all. Hubba hubba!

It was like the chemicals in my body readjusted, and my dam of tension released. I curled into his tan chest, and weeks and months of pent-up worry rolled down my cheeks. His eyes met mine. "We were always okay. We are always going to be okay."

Just between us, rejection is a huge deal. I understand because I live afraid of it every day, but I push forward anyway. Sometimes, we have to stare down our fears and risk rejection. Why? Because on the other side of fear is freedom! Sweet, spacious freedom. Had Anthony and I not been able to go through with it, I would have felt rejected. I would have made a mountain out of a molehill, but I would have survived. We would have survived. And we would have found our way back to joy.

**Sometimes, we have to stare down
our fears and risk rejection.**

Hope for Navigating—Joy

Guided by Dr. Brene Brown's *The Gifts of Imperfection*, I sat down and worked on my "dream" and "joy and meaning" lists. What dreams did I want for my life, and what brought me joy and meaning?

Mostly predictable answers occupied my dream list: big house, fancy car, Elizabeth Taylor's jewelry collection. But it also included filling auditoriums full of people for public speaking, having a best-selling book on the market, and having access to Jane Fonda's plastic surgeon. Half the things on my dream list could be checked off by money, while the other half could be checked off by hard work.

Then I started on the joy and meaning list, which took a little longer. I sat with a hot cup of coffee and searched. What brings me joy? What helps me feel meaning? The list began to form in my mind. I feel joy and meaning when:

- I teach and coach and have a positive impact on others.
- I am connected with friends and family.
- I am learning and growing.
- I am laughing/smiling and bringing laughter/smiles.
- I am clapping, singing, and dancing.
- I travel and learn about other parts of the world.
- I am appreciative of nature.
- I am devoted to God.
- I treat my body well.
- I give love and receive love.
- I give those in my life the best I have to offer, especially my husband and daughter.

I reviewed the simplicity of my list in surprise. *Could it all really be that simple?* Could I *already* have joy and meaning? No way. I looked at the list again. Nowhere did I write, *I feel joy and meaning when I buy new clothes, or when I spend a lot of money, or when I have more Instagram followers than anyone else.* Nowhere did I write, *I feel joy and meaning when others envy my car or when I am able to purchase designer duds.* I realized the things that bring me joy and meaning were *already* in my life. It's easy to confuse realizing our dreams with discovering our joy.

If it gives you joy and meaning to be the best lawyer around, do it. If it gives you joy and meaning to cuddle with your partner for six hours on Saturday, do it. If it gives you joy and meaning to take all your spending money and donate it to an animal shelter instead of spending it on a new winter coat, do it. Let's focus our energy on the things that fill our hearts and settle our souls. Can we all agree that when it comes to joy and meaning, *more is more?*

**I realized the things that bring me joy
and meaning were *already* in my life. It's easy
to confuse realizing our dreams
with discovering our joy.**

Today will be filled with choices. And each decision will get us closer to the joy-filled life we want, or it will take us further from it. Let's identify what lights us up and what makes us come alive. Then, let's seek it in ways large and small—in ways that make money, and even ways that don't. Let's aim to fill our lives with joy and meaning from sun up to sun down. The people, situations, and activities that bring us joy, meaning, and a sense of purpose are powerful; they will get us out of bed in the morning, thrilled that another day is upon us. Let's be honest about who we are and what we need. The rest tends to work itself out.

ciety's blueprint of a great life wash over us; there is no
a magazine-worthy life. The prize, the true glory, comes
hat is fully experienced and fully poured out—a life that
ateful existed. Let's be careful not to compare ourselves
to others. Let's breathe in deeply and take a look around—our lives are
chock-full of blessings and fortune.

"Joy is waiting for you, and the door is unlocked."
—Pete Holmes

Trail Journal

When was the last time you felt pure joy?

nature — California, March 2018

How would your life change if your decisions were fueled by joy as an outcome?

What is something that makes you feel fully alive?

Dancing + teaching dance

Chapter 13

CHANGE IN CARE

From a few months before the pregnancy until halfway through the pregnancy, I received all sorts of prenatal care. I had experienced an anatomy scan, where we saw our baby girl up close. I had had blood tests, ultrasounds, sonograms, nasty glucose testing, and even a CVS. I was under spectacular care from my OB/GYN in South Texas, from a maternal fetal medicine specialist, and even from my Houston OB/GYN, but now I needed to find care in Austin.

In my search, birthing centers interested me. As far as I knew, birthing centers were a pleasant, homelike environment where ladies gave birth. I had a healthy and active pregnancy. I walked, did yoga, and swam. I even attended cycling classes. *Why wouldn't my body cooperate and open right up?* My body was strong and so was the baby's, making us perfect candidates for a birthing center. I knew my mom had given birth to my two brothers and me vaginally, with no pain medication, and I quite admired her for it—so much so that I had ambitions to do the same.

I called around to a few places to figure out if a birthing center was really for us. Eventually, I stumbled upon a birthing center in downtown Austin. I liked the vibe of the staff over the phone, so I pursued it further. We were still unpacking our cardboard boxes when the day arrived for my first appointment.

I drove up, parked on the street, paid the meter, and walked inside. *Metered parking! Women labored and someone was worried about metered parking?* Anyway, it had all the makings of a house: four bedrooms, creaky wood floors, a working kitchen, and old smelly chairs in the foyer (now lobby). It was a house, and women had babies in it. I couldn't get over it.

My initial meeting was with a midwife and an apprentice. Their office (formerly a bedroom) was made up of a simple desk, a computer, and a filing cabinet, but there were also tribal statues, old worn pillows, and a creaky day bed. They sat in chairs, and I sat on the daybed. I was a *long* way from the Houston medical center.

They evaluated my charts and my health to see if I had any issues that would make me a high-risk patient. They decided they were comfortable taking me on, and I decided I was comfortable delivering our baby at a birthing center. Our midwives used technology sparingly, and as June progressed and my belly got bigger, I missed being able to check in on our baby via sonogram. My appointments consisted of peeing in a cup, checking my pulse and blood pressure, and feeling around for the baby. No fancy machines and no listening to her heartbeat. It was a real change, but I was pleased to have found care so quickly. We were in business!

Just Between Us

I thought of labor as an adventure, an obstacle course of sorts. I was a Tough Mudder, for goodness' sake. I had rappelled down a thirty-two-story building, I had jumped out of a plane, and I had had sex with my husband despite my enormous belly! I knew I could give birth at a birthing center, no problem. I was going to give birth without the help of medical staff or pain intervention. I knew I was awesome, and everything was going to work out perfectly. But just between us … sometimes life turns when you least expect it.

Ampairsing!

Hope for Navigating—Rolling with the Punches

Borrowed from the boxing world, *rolling with the punches* implies that one is quick on his feet, flexible, and able to absorb the force of a blow. Of course, the ability to skillfully avoid a direct hit by bobbing and weaving is preferable, but every boxer understands that contact is inevitable. Smart boxers learn to *roll with the punches.* They quite literally move their body in the direction of the hit to lessen the force of impact. Figuratively, rolling with the punches involves adjusting to events as they happen. Rolling with the punches is about choosing fluidity over resistance.

Much of the time, change is difficult because it moves us away from familiarity. We've gotten used to a certain set of girlfriends; we have a rhythm with them. Or we have gotten used to dating our boyfriend, but he isn't always forthright, and we're holding out hope he will love our children as much as we do. Or, we always do big sugar-laden cakes for family members' birthdays, so how can we ever learn to celebrate without CAKE?! The list goes on and on. Right?

Sometimes we know we deserve better, but we're afraid of making changes because it will take actual effort. Yes, the bad news is it *will* take *actual* effort. But the good news is that a lighter heart, and a more joyful existence, is on the other side of that effort.

As the brilliant Tina Fey says, "Say 'yes,' and figure it out afterward." Not that we need to be saying "yes" to *everything.* But how many things do we say "no" to because it will throw off our schedule, or because it's a new endeavor and we're afraid of being beginners, or because we don't want to go somewhere by ourselves? Or, if you're like me, you don't want to pack and unpack an entire home while being seven months pregnant!

There are things that we must admittedly say "no" to, and there are things that are begging to be done. Moves that are waiting to made. Jobs that are ready to be thrown out the window. Relationships that are waiting for a shakeup. There are things we want or need to do, and yet we say "no" because of logistics. Girlfriend, if logistics is all that's in the way, say YES—and figure out the rest afterward.

When we feel like we are skimming the surface of our lives and want more depth, it is there for the taking. Will it involve rolling with the punches? Inevitably. But will we love our lives more afterward? Heck YES.

Rolling with the punches is about choosing fluidity over resistance.

"Whatever is flexible and flowing will tend to grow;
whatever is rigid and blocked will wither and die."
—Tao Te Ching

yep!

Living things move. They grow.

Trail Journal

What happens when you are presented with change?

What is the last thing you said YES to?

Would it benefit your life if you were more flexible?

We all
have to captain
our
own ships

Chapter 14

CHANGE IN WORK

I entered my third trimester, which meant the end of my traveling outside of Austin. Under midwife's orders, I was no longer allowed to drive to South Texas for work, so telecommuting was the extent of my work contribution. I felt shackled.

I wanted to figure out my next step, workwise, to be fair to my parents' company and to maintain my peace of mind. I needed to have a good sense of direction. *Would I be a stay-at-home mama? Would I try to travel with the baby and continue working? What did that look like? Would I want to work more than ever, or would I want to work less?* Deciding whether or not to work outside the home weighed on me heavily.

Like a squirrel collects nuts, I collected anecdotes from women I trusted. I asked them what their lives were like and what they would do differently if given the opportunity. I observed moms around me and asked them how they juggled work, kids, and their personal lives. Some ladies worked full-time outside the home, and some didn't work outside the home at all. Some were financially stretched once they placed their child in daycare, and some moms chose not to put their children in daycare at all. Some moms with master's level educations chose to stay at home full-time with occasional help. As I searched, I hoped to find a one-size-fits-all answer, but I never did. *Right! Yep. There isnt one.*

If I did continue working outside the home, a lot of time management and organization was going to have to be put in place. The planner in me would be tested: *How would I get to South Texas? Would my baby magically sleep for a five-hour drive? How would I work during the day? Where would we stay? Who would help us?* Or, would I have to leave my job with my parents' company? Leaving had some downsides, the biggest being I would see my family much less. I had always worked with my family in one way or another, and not doing so would feel strange. *If I left my position, would I be letting my family down?* Another downside of leaving was that I would have less to hang my hat on. *How would I identify? Would I just be a stay-at-home mom?* It also meant I would not earn an income. I would be fully financially dependent on my husband. And as an independent woman, full financial dependence frightened me. *Where would I get the money I wanted to spend? Would I have an allowance? How was this going to work?* And if I couldn't hang my hat on work, how was I going to find worth? I found worth in working!

Would I work? Would I not work? Would I work part-time? Would working be more important to me than before or less important? Would I not care at all? Would I feel less motivated to write, or would I feel more motivated?

There were so many questions that I wanted to answer *now*, but as my pregnancy progressed, my hormones skyrocketed, which rendered me useless. I mean, one day my dad (my boss) sent me an email, and I almost resigned my position because I was so enraged. HORMONES. I knew then that I was ill equipped to operate heavy machinery, so I tabled all decision-making until post-pregnancy. I didn't want to pressure myself to make a decision and then change my mind a few months down the road. I was dog-tired, temperamental, and unable to make clear-cut decisions. Even choosing where to eat dinner was rough!

However, in spite of being decisive about one thing—NOT making decisions—I still felt the mounting pressure to determine what kind of woman and mom I wanted to be. *Would I work or would I stay home?*

Just Between Us

I wanted to have it all figured out. And I wanted to have it all figured out on my timetable—as if I could check a box and it would be all done.

Deciding whether or not to change my work situation was enormous. I had spent my entire life working, so *not* working was foreign to me. Ever since I had been able to contribute, I had. Ever since I had been able to earn an income, I had. For me, money equaled independence, a leg to stand on, and I was terrified of what would happen if that were taken away. I knew my husband loved me, and I knew I was safe, but I felt vulnerable. And when you're pregnant, *feelings RULE all*.

Just between us, when you are pregnant, there are a *lot* of changes going on in your body and mind. With the arrival of the baby come unexpected twists and turns. There is enough to learn and to adjust around without adding the pressure of more life changes—or the pressure of deciding on who you think you should be.

Just between us, it's okay to feel it out and take your time. However, some of us will feel like we don't have the luxury of taking our time or making choices, but somehow, we do. Even if we choose to stay in our jobs or apartments or living situations until we can get our head above water, or until the baby arrives, or until the baby is six months old, that in itself is a choice. When we take ownership of the choice, the tone of our life changes.

What a wonderful opportunity that you get to build the life you *want*! Do what works for you. You have all the tools to make the right decisions. Get still, pray, and listen to your intuition.

Hope for Navigating—Shifting Roles

I was talking with my girlfriend once, during our walk around the park, and I asked her how she took the leap of leaving a nine-to-five job to pursue work in the creative arts. Since she had a newborn and no job lined up, I thought her move was fantastically courageous. She went on to tell me how she had resolute faith that she would figure it out. She didn't know what the plan would be or what it would look like—but she knew she could. She had faith in her*self*.

Faith is extraordinarily important when we are shifting roles—whether from job to job or independent career woman to domesticated motherhood. Like my friend who switched career paths, I knew that being part of a marriage and entering into motherhood was an uncharted road, a trail yet to be discovered. But I also knew that I was safe, I was loved, and if I tried my best, I would find my way.

What I've learned about characters who do big things is that they are not necessarily fearless while they shift from one role to the next; rather, they are simply confident in their ability to handle whatever uncertainties or trials come their way. It's not that they aren't scared—it's that they use their high expectations, unbridled optimism, and channeled fears to propel them forward.

We've all seen her—you know, the lady sitting at the coffee shop, perfectly prim, that looks like she's got it all figured out. But my bet is that she doesn't. She may appear confident, put-together, and self-assured on the outside, but there are times she struggles, just like we do, on the inside. There are moments she doubts herself, looking around, wishing she had the answers.

We shouldn't be intimidated by anyone who *looks* like they have it all together—they don't. None of us do. But what we *do* have is the capacity to be supportive and help one another out along the way.

At some point on each of our trails, we try our hands at new relationships, old relationships, shifting family dynamics, burgeoning careers, stale vocations, new moms groups ... and we all fumble. *But*, thankfully, we all have the ability to see those experiences through, even if seeing them through takes exponentially longer than we originally thought. After all, "Identity is never static, always in the making and never made" (anonymous).

> *"Try not to resist the changes that come your way. Instead, let life live through you. And do not worry that your life is turning upside down. How do you know that the side you are used to is better than the one to come?"*
> *—Rumi*

Trail Journal

Would you identify yourself as career-oriented?

yes.

Is pursuing a career important to you? Why?

security, breed, opportunity to see family/friends who are not here.

Is there a career shift you'd like to make if given the opportunity?

yes.

writing books full time, I think.

Chapter 15 ~what a chapter.~

PREPARATION

By all accounts, I experienced all the typical stages of pregnancy. Early on, I was afraid of miscarrying, then I had body image issues, and then my husband and I had a blip in our sex life. My boob size increased (twice), and then I experienced swelling (my toes resembling sausages). I also experienced emotional sensitivity (to be very polite about it) and a swing in hormones often … okay, maybe every day. Any misuse of a single word would send me spinning. "Maybe? What do you mean, *maybe?* I'm not pretty? So you think I'm not pretty?" Gold medal to my steadfast husband.

Our baby's due date was nearing, and I moved on to the next typical phase of pregnancy: nesting. I made lists and let my OCD loose. The best I could tell, once the baby arrived, it was going to be all hands on deck. People told me how poopy diapers and breast milk would be flying, so I wanted to be as prepared as possible (famous last words). I figured that the more prepared our home was on the front end, the calmer I would be on the back end. As her arrival date neared, activities ramped up, and I had a list of things I wanted to accomplish. The month before her due date was chock-full of baby preparation.

Infant CPR

First on the list was attending an infant CPR class. And just after our class began, I knew that I didn't know a thing. "Poison control number here. 9-1-1 here. Thirty chest presses … sternum … is the baby blue or breathing? And don't forget—don't panic!" There must have been twenty people in class, and I thought—*Is everyone getting this? I hope I never have to use this. How does any child ever survive with all the possible things that can go wrong?* My husband and I completed the class, and even though I didn't feel like an ace, I felt I had enough working knowledge to keep me calm during an emergency situation.

Breastfeeding Basics

After "learning" about infant CPR, I attended a breastfeeding basics class. Beyond putting the baby to my chest, I had no idea how nursing worked. *How was I supposed to hold the baby? How would I know if the baby was getting enough milk? How often was I going to have to do this thing they call breastfeeding?* I had never seen anyone breastfeed, so it was a foreign concept. I walked into the class ready to take notes. I wanted the lactation consultant to teach me all she knew. The instructor taught us how to hold and burp the baby and what the normal process looked like. She even taught us how to hand-express milk. With my hand raised, I asked, "What happens when our baby is freaking out at three in the morning?" I had visions of not being able to get the baby to latch; what if she had nipple confusion and became hysterical with hunger pangs? I was expecting the absolute worst. "You do your best, and you call us in the morning." *Great! No help there!*

As far as I was concerned, her answer was the worst possible one. I knew I'd be able to handle problems during the light of day. I was concerned about problems occurring *after business hours,* when customer service was closed and the moon was out. I left feeling more knowledgeable about breastfeeding, but also hoping that the breastfeeding fairies would have it in their hearts to show me mercy and allow it all to go smoothly. I dreaded a three o-clock in the morning wailing session. I wanted someone to call in case of a breastfeeding emergency.

I was in the throes of pregnancy, and I was faced with certain stressful doom, so—in the way a basketball coach pieces together a championship ball team—I pieced together a championship labor team.

Lactation Consultant

Before being pregnant, I filed lactation consultants in my mind as professionals hired by new moms who had a little extra money to spend. *Couldn't they figure it out themselves?* Hiring a lactation consultant seemed luxurious and totally unnecessary … until I thought I needed one. Then, it was an *absolute* necessity.

On a sunny July afternoon, I called a lactation consultant, and when she picked up, I heard a sweet-sounding voice. I introduced myself and told her I had about a month until the baby arrived.

"Ok, just call me if an issue arises. You don't need to book me in advance. You'll be fine, and so will your baby. You probably won't ever need to call me."

Why wouldn't I need her? What kind of business lady was she?

"Your level of preparedness and your willingness to tackle this one month ahead of time tells me you'll be fine. Willingness is most of the battle."

Nice! Maybe we *would* be okay.

Birthing Class

Before each birthing center appointment, I'd sit in the hot, musty lobby, waiting to be called in for my checkup. It aggravated me that they didn't splurge on keeping the thermostat at seventy-five degrees. They held the temperature at a strong, jungle-like seventy-eight degrees, and my swollen ankles, fingers, and toes were pissed about it. The lobby was filled with makeshift announcement stations that advertised baby photographers, massage therapists, acupuncturists, and childbirth classes.

Since I knew I didn't know anything about childbirth, I signed us up for birthing classes with Summer Miller. Anthony and I took to her right away. She was able to answer questions for couples who were having traditional hospital births, birthing center births, and home births. She knew her stuff, and we could tell. She took us through topics such as how I would know I was in labor, ways Anthony could be of assistance, and natural pain management.

During our last class, we watched birthing videos, and the graphic content sent me tumbling over the edge. Seemingly normal women were transformed into tribal-like women. They swayed from side to side, grunted from guttural places, and zoned out to the point where they were unable to see what was going on around them. They looked and sounded weird. Some labored with their hair a mess, or worse, with family and friends hovering around, lending helping hands. And they were in so much pain that zoning out seemed to be their only option, which also made me extremely uncomfortable.

I wanted to have a natural birth, *and* I wanted to look good doing it. I wanted the baby to be safe, but I didn't want messy hair, and I didn't want to leak buckets of sweat. I didn't want to be in—or even *appear* in—distress. I wanted to be calm and collected, wearing just the right birthing gown. I wanted everyone to know just how strong I was, and I wanted them to be impressed. The ladies in birthing videos did not exhibit the type of labor I wanted to experience.

Watching the videos prompted me to think about exactly how I wanted my labor to play out. What did I want to wear? I was hoping against hope that no one would force me to labor braless. Did I want to be sitting or squatting? Did I want to have a water birth or music playing?

Each couple in our birthing class had their own set of questions; however, most of them did not pertain to us. The yuppie couple was choosing to have a hospital birth, and the hippie couple was choosing to have a home birth. We were smack in the middle with a birthing center birth.

After hearing questions from the other two couples, I was glad we weren't going to be in *those* situations. We weren't going to have to deal with unnecessary, evil medication. We were not going to deal with a possible C-section or epidurals or IVs. I was going to labor, and it was going to be difficult, but I was going to be fine.

Birthing Center Class

Midway through July, Anthony and I took another birthing class, but this one was mandatory and presented by the midwives at our birthing center.

We arrived on a Saturday morning for the three-hour class and piled into a room. As I looked around and sized up the other students, I could tell we were the odd couple out. Everyone else was so laid back, with their tattoos and piercings and bohemian clothing. I, on the contrary, was *not* laid back and became increasingly less so as the class progressed.

Midway through our morning together, a student asked, "If we go into labor at the same time as another birthing center client, will we each have our own labor team?" This question seemed preposterous to me. *Of course, lady! This isn't 1904.*

The owner of the birthing center, who was teaching the class, replied, "No. There will only be one team. So, if two ladies go into labor at the same time, the midwife will hop back and forth between rooms." She continued, assuring us that the likelihood of two ladies laboring at the same time was slim.

hahahahaha

But it was too late; I didn't care what she said after the word, "NO." *Are you freaking kidding me? If I'm in labor, I may have to share my already thin support?* I was appalled and thought it was poor form on their part not to share this information with patients up front. I had never been pregnant before, much less labored before, so there were a slew of questions I just didn't know to ask.

Anthony and I left that class annoyed and began searching for solutions.

Cord Blood Banking

When we signed up with our birthing center, we asked them if capturing cord blood was a service they provided. They assured us they did.

Cord blood banking involves a medical professional extracting blood and tissue from the umbilical cord just after a birth, then cryogenically freezing and storing it. The extracted blood and tissue are rich in value. They can be used to help heal certain diseases should the child be faced with them later in life. Having cord blood and tissue as a resource seemed like a very good idea to us, and we opted to have the procedure performed.

On the heels of being told I might have to share a birthing team, I brought up the cord blood collection as I wanted to get a plan in place, but I was met with total ambiguity.

"Well, we're not sure. We can't guarantee 100 percent that we'll be able to collect cord blood. We're 95 percent certain we can, but we may not have enough hands in the room. There will be a midwife and an apprentice in the room, and their main concerns will be the health of the mom and baby."

No shit. Of course the priorities are the baby's health and the mom's health.

I wanted to be absolutely certain the midwives could and would, in fact, recover cord blood and tissue. In their explanation to me, the midwives threw around phrases like *almost sure* and *probably.* I didn't want to leave anything to chance. I wanted a definitive, resounding *yes.*

At our next appointment, Anthony marched in and addressed the elephant in the room: why were they being squirmy about the cord blood collection? The midwives confessed to being philosophically opposed to the idea of cord blood banking. It was their opinion that taking blood from the umbilical cord was really taking it from the baby. Anthony thanked them for their opinion and told them that he and I were in charge; we still wanted to collect cord blood.

To eliminate any ambiguity, Anthony and I decided to hire an additional midwife. She would be in the room during labor, and her sole responsibility was to collect the baby's cord blood.

Doula

During my last month of pregnancy, I began to doubt my birthing center decision. It seemed as if pitfalls loomed around every corner.

The due date was approaching quickly, and it was too late to scrap our birthing center plan, so we asked Summer to be our doula and bring ease to the experience. She was knowledgeable, pleasant, informative, and supportive—just the type of person I wanted on my side. She had worked with our midwives before, and I knew she'd be able to mend the fence enough to get us through the birth. When she agreed to be our doula, I jumped for joy! (But not too high, because I was pregnant, of course.) I knew she would support our decisions and find ways to get our needs met without judgment.

Placenta

I was in my third trimester when a friend mentioned placenta encapsulation. I knew what a placenta was, but I wasn't sure how it could be encapsulated. Finding the answer made my stomach turn. Placenta encapsulation involves dehydrating the delivered placenta, like a piece of meat. Once it's dried, it's cut up into pieces resembling beef jerky. The pieces are pulverized, mixed with herbs, and placed into vitamin capsules. Then they are ready for consumption, just like any other vitamin.

It sounded absolutely disgusting, but then I read that ingesting the placenta helps level out hormonal swings post-childbirth. Postpartum depression did not run in my family, but I knew that I experienced anxiety, and so I had an inkling I might experience it. To combat that possibility, I agreed to the placenta encapsulation.

I searched and found a lady who offered placenta encapsulation. "Reserving" her service was quite informal, considering I was asking her to come to the birthing center, pick up an ORGAN, prepare it, and then return it to me. *What if she packed my pills with someone else's placenta? Who was to say she would include a placenta at all? What if she only filled the vitamin capsules with herbs?* There was no licensing, no regulation ... just trust. I would not be able to prove a thing—I signed up anyway. Anything that would move me away from postpartum depression was a friend of mine.

Help After Baby

Off the bat, hiring a night nurse sounded extravagant. But the more time I had to think about all the things that could go wrong, the more I warmed to the idea of a night nurse. I didn't have friends or family close by who could help with the baby, so I knew I would need some kind of assistance. I just wasn't sure what it would look like. In preparation, I wanted to line up a night nurse, just as I had done with the lactation consultant. In my research, I found that they charged upwards of $20 an hour, with a minimum of six hours! Sticker shock. On the one hand, I didn't want to pay $120 per night; but on the other hand, I absolutely wanted someone worth $20 an hour, someone who knew what they were doing and could pull from a breadth of experience. I bookmarked the information and resolved that I'd reach for a night nurse in case of emergency.

Finally, my all-star labor and postpartum team was assembled.

While gathering my team, I also prepared our home. With the help of good friends, mommy blogs, and Amazon, I purchased everything I could possibly need. All the goodies I purchased would help me labor at home through the early stages and later at the birthing center. I also had items that would help me recover at home.

Our birthing center encouraged us to labor at home for as long as possible; laboring in the comforts of home was more pleasant than laboring in an unfamiliar room, so we heeded their advice and established a game plan. We strategized where we would labor and with what we would labor. We'd use a birthing ball to open up my hips, tennis balls to rub on my lower back, and peppermint oil on washcloths to combat the sweating. *We were prepared!* I packed our "go-time" bags with clothes, snacks, extra cell phone chargers, and even motivational wall signs to help me through labor. If someone suggested it, I packed it. It mattered not that each bag went from a duffle to a full-on suitcase. Preparedness equaled calmness.

To ease the recovery process at home, I assembled homeopathic remedy kits for each bathroom. Each box was stocked with witch hazel, lavender, sanitary pads, water bottles, wipes, sitz bath salts, creams … you name it, I had it. I also stocked up on herbal teas, stretchy clothing, and a postpartum belly band to help support my core. I prepared (and purchased) like a tornado was on its way. I didn't want to be knee-deep in baby cries and wishing that I had taken one extra trip to the store.

A few weeks before her due date, I was as ready as I would ever be. I had taken classes, learned all I could, thought out a strategy, and assembled a team. I had loaded the house with food and goodies, and I had cleared our schedules for August. I was on my toes and ready to go.

Just Between Us

Just between us, the closer the due date came, the more I tensed up. Things were no longer hypothetical; they were real. The baby was coming, and she was going to have to *exit my body.* I began to fret about things large and small; nothing was safe. My mind spun all day, every day. Hormones ran my life. At every turn, someone seemed to be poking holes into my perfect plan, and it was irritating.

Every professional I contacted was an effort on my part to prepare myself for bringing a new life into the world and then for responsibly raising her. I assembled a team because that's what made me feel comfortable. My way worked for me—mostly. But my way is not the only way! If you feel comfortable going at it alone, or with your partner, or with your partner and your mom, then by all means do it. If you want your mom to join you, ask! If you want everyone possible to help, have them help! Your mama intuition will guide you. Millions of years of evolution are on your side. If you are thinking about the well-being of your child before he/she is even born, you're already spectacular.

Laboring is an immensely personal process. Beyond the smaller details of who you want in the room and what you want to snack on, there is a much larger picture. If you are laboring, God has partnered with you to bring new life into the world. Your family is about to expand. Cell by cell, your body has miraculously created life. And—spoiler alert—labor is not the end! Your heart and body will continue to care for your child, forever more. Laboring and everything that accompanies it should be as close as possible to what you and your partner deem favorable.

Just between us, I thought I would only be praiseworthy if I cared for our daughter alone. If I enlisted the help of a nanny or a night nurse, would I be wussing out? I questioned whether anyone would be proud of me. I questioned if I was cheating the system by having help. *Wasn't I supposed to suffer long sleepless nights? Would I really earn my Mom Badge if I had a night nurse helping?* Sometimes I get stuck because I am worried about how my life *looks*; I am not focused on how my life *feels*.

**Sometimes I get stuck because I am worried
about how my life *looks*; I am not focused on
how my life feels.**

Hope for Navigating—Being In the Weeds

When I was eighteen and in college, I put on a matronly grey suit and two-inch black pumps and interviewed for a hostess position at a high-energy, see-and-be-seen kind of restaurant in downtown Austin. The general manager hired me on the spot: "Welcome to the top of the mountain," he said as he shook my hand.

Because we were an overachieving team, we were taught to book more reservations than we had seats available, and then we would "dance." Some tables would clear before their estimated two-hour dinner, so we'd be able to fit in other guests. Sometimes, the governor of Texas would arrive unannounced, and we'd have to finagle his favorite table from unassuming customers. Sometimes Reese Witherspoon would walk in the door, and we'd all melt. Most of the time, I was so busy that I would not only hostess, but I would bus tables or run food or clean the bathroom. All hands on deck, all the time.

When we're in the weeds, and overwhelmed, let's slow down and *find our calm*. It's in the slowing down that we then gain a sense of clarity.

It was there in that new, adrenaline-pumping environment that I learned what it was to be "in the weeds." In the service industry, we use this term to mean *"REALLY busy—I'm doing all I can to stay afloat."*

When we are in life's weeds, we often get tense, unpleasant to be around, grouchy, and sometimes quite loud about it. (Oops.) This never does any good and makes things infinitely more unmanageable.

If we are in a constant state of alarm, our brains keep our bodies at high alert, hearts racing, blood pressure soaring, and sympathetic nervous system (*fight-flight-freeze*) firing—no good for anyone.

in the weeds, and overwhelmed, let's slow down and *find*
in the slowing down that we then gain a sense of clarity.
n is *powerful.* When we are calm, we keep our frontal
lobe—the part of our brain responsible for higher-level thinking and
decision-making—engaged. *that right.*

When we're challenged and have an overwhelming amount of work, to-do
lists, or projects, let's take a moment to stop and breathe, blow off some
steam with some fun and laughter, grab a glass of wine, and get ourselves
to a place of calm. If we can remain calm on both the outside (physically)
and inside (mentally), we're more likely to make better decisions and get
the outcome we desire.

**It's in the slowing down that we then gain a
sense of clarity. Keeping calm is powerful.**

"When you feel the need to speed up, slow down."
–African Proverb

Trail Journal

When was the last time you felt like you were in the weeds?

Does being in the weeds bother you or motivate you?

Can you see how remaining calm while in the weeds would make a difference for the better?

Chapter 16

WAITING FOR DELIVERY

Two weeks before the baby's due date, I devoted myself to preparing my body for labor. I swam, squatted, opened my hips, and stretched. I ate oatmeal and flax seeds and drank uterus-ripening tea. I even resorted to sex. (Sex at forty weeks pregnant is WHOA!) Every day, I wholeheartedly tried to prepare myself for labor, and every day I experienced two to three hours of contractions. It was exhausting.

On the one hand, I didn't want to rush the baby, but on the other hand, I was feeling physically pushed to my limit. I had lost some sensation in my fingers and toes due to poor circulation, and her feet were pressed against my lungs, which made it difficult to breathe. Even the simple act of eating became a source of stress. I *wanted* to eat, but my stomach was pancaked against my lungs, and it made for an uncomfortable experience. I *wanted* to rest, but I could never find a position comfortable enough to sleep. When I stood, blood pooled in my ankles and feet, and when I sat, my belly scrunched and tightened my hips. Surprisingly, lying down felt just as terrible! When I laid down, blood rushed to my head and the veins in my neck swelled; I felt like my head was about to explode. I couldn't even cuddle with my husband because I couldn't manage to get enough oxygen while in a prone position. Woe is me. *Yhus —LOL!*

To help my body manage the intense physical stress of pregnancy, I frequented a chiropractor and acupuncturist. Both ladies also did their *A Justin recommended this too.*

best to prepare my body for labor. They aligned my hips, adjusted my neck, opened meridians, and aggressively stimulated pressure points. My body was ready. Of course, the baby was going to arrive on her August 9 due date.

So there I was, August 3, August 4 … nothing. August 5, August 6, August 7 … nothing. Friday, August 8 … something! I woke up in the middle of the night because I had to poop. POOP! *What in the world?* I walked to the bathroom, head spinning and abdominal area cramping. It was a very strange sensation. I knew that loose bowels were an early sign of labor, and so I mentally prepared for the day ahead. My husband and I were on high alert. Our baby was already overachieving so she would without a doubt be among the 5 percent of babies that arrive on their estimated due date.

Naturally, I insisted on shopping. I wanted to be stocked up with everything I could need for weeks. Never mind that we were already stocked; I wanted to be MORE stocked. *Hormones.* After our shopping trip, I prudently stayed hydrated, fed, and rested. *Put me in, coach. Put me in!* I was ready, I was ready, I was ready … then all of a sudden, the sun turned from bright yellow to deep orange, and the moon rose. Her due date had passed.

The next day, Sunday, I went to church and did the only thing I knew to do: I prayed to God for patience. The two weeks leading up to our baby's due date had been filled with anticipation, dejection, and confinement. If I was going to hold on to the bit of sanity I had left, I had to release the expectancy of labor. It didn't do anybody any good for me to be stressed out about the baby's late arrival. I didn't need any extra pressure. I figured it was best to keep fighting the good fight, but also to be peaceful knowing she would arrive when she was ready.

Just Between Us

I was pregnant, and my husband may not have known he was signing up to be my main support system, but he absolutely was, and I needed every bit he could offer.

He was remarkably attentive, calling every few hours from his downtown office to make sure I knew that my health and the safety of our baby and me were his top priority. He encouraged me to seek out the best care we could access. There were endless vitamins, massages, and chiropractic and acupuncture appointments. He attended birthing classes with me—to learn, but also to show his support. And above all, he was steady in his love for me. Through every mood swing (okay, *most* mood swings), he was calm. Through every crying session, he was understanding. Through my body image woes, he was supportive and complimentary. He was the best husband I could ask for.

I thank God I paid attention to my intuition on our first date and had the wherewithal to not screw it all up. I thank God for blessing me with such a strong and wholehearted man, one who has loved and continues to love me so honestly and completely.

Just between us, the space in between my ears was a hot-mangled mess. I'm sure I was a lot to handle. But the edges were softened on the rough days because I had a champion of a husband at my side.

Hope for Navigating—Patience

I come from a long line of citrus and vegetable farmers; my great grandpa was a farmer, my grandpa was a farmer, and my dad is a farmer. I grew up learning to prepare and then to wait in expectancy. Well before the harvest is to happen, the land is tilled and prepared. Some years call for planting seedlings, while others call for maximizing the output of more mature plants. Farmers aim to provide the best growing environment for their crop, and then they wait, hoping Mother Nature will be on their side.

Farmers willingly tether themselves to nature. They may walk the rows of orchards, checking on the soil and irrigation as the work is done beneath the ground, but ultimately, the product of their sowing is somewhat out of their hands. Wisely, most farmers, instead of waiting impatiently, intertwine patience and expectancy for those first signs of life and an abundant crop. "Adopt the pace of nature, her secret is patience."[15] If farmers dug up in doubt what they planted in faith,[16] they would drive themselves mad.

If we are willing to let go of the *how* and *when*, patience rewards us with ease.

We have been conditioned to get what we want—immediately. As consumers, we have everything at our fingertips. From a new dinner recipe, to learning what planet is orbiting the earth, to getting our groceries delivered, we are accustomed to instant gratification. All that convenience is well and good, but when we take this expectation for instant gratification and apply it to our interior lives, we miss out. We end up forgoing opportunities to practice gratitude, to be more mindful, and to truly experience the gritty nature of growth that only comes *through* the discomfort of waiting.

Writer Susan Gale says, "The longer you have to wait for something, the more you will appreciate it when it finally arrives. The harder you have to fight for something, the more priceless it will become once you achieve it. And the more pain you have to endure on your journey, the sweeter the arrival at your destination. All good things are worth waiting for and worth fighting for."

Whatever we plant in our lives—new career opportunities, new relationships, new community initiatives—let's plant it with patience and expectancy. We may not have control of the circumstances in our lives, but we do have control over where we focus our attention, and what kind of energy we give that focus.

that's right!

If we are willing to let go of the _how_ and _when_, patience rewards us with ease.

"Waiting is the hardest work of hope."
—Lewis Smedes

Trail Journal

What's your relationship with patience like?

Bad girl, we aint friends.

Describe a time in your life when you were forced into waiting.

Right now, anyway.

How do you think waiting for what you wanted impacted you?

Ugh.
Longing
It grows.

Chapter 17

CHANGE IN PLAN

The Monday *after* my due date, I went in for my weekly checkup at the birthing center. I was at forty weeks and two days' gestation.

"We've been thinking about you! We were sure you were going to go into labor yesterday!"

The night before, there had been a super moon. And since full moons are known to spur ladies on the cusp of labor, everyone (including me) was sure I would go into labor. Well, I didn't.

The midwives encouraged me to be patient and assured me that all my efforts were going to pay off. They also advised that I get a biophysical profile to check the baby's position, her estimated weight, and the level of amniotic fluid. The birthing center did not have in-office technology capable of doing this test, so they sent me to a doctor's office. I was elated that I'd be able to catch a glimpse of our baby again.

I continued to squat, swim, and eat foods said to induce labor. I even asked both my chiropractor and acupuncturist to push the envelope with their treatments. I was nearing forty-one weeks, and I knew the longer the baby took to arrive, the more complications were possible.

On the day of the biophysical profile, we walked into the examination room, and I felt grateful to be surrounded by medical technology. *Why would I EVER have deprived myself of this comfort?* Anthony held my freshly manicured hand while the nurse rubbed warm gel over my belly. And after a few minutes, we saw her. "There you are!" She was head down, heart beating strong, estimated at 8.2 pounds, and in the perfect position. Her living quarters were holding up just fine, and there was no reason to induce labor.

It seemed everyone had their own version of "This will do the trick." *Walk on a topographical surface.* Someone suggested that, at forty-one weeks pregnant, I go take a hike! *Make eggplant parmigiana, from scratch.* I did. *Eat eggplant parmigiana, and then go take a ride in a jeep over a bumpy surface. Do squats. Do yoga. Have sex. Drink castor oil!* One day, as I picked up some dinner to go, a man yelled at me from across the restaurant, "Mexican food!" I just laughed. My body was ready, but she wasn't. Or was it the other way around? I didn't know anymore, but I *did* know that I didn't want to rush her. She would come in her own time.

The days rolled into one another, and I waddled into my Monday appointment at the birthing center, forty-one weeks and three days pregnant. They couldn't believe I was still pregnant, so they gave me two options. The first option was to try "natural" inducement, which included having my membranes swiped (which was mildly effective and horribly painful), drinking castor oil, and being hooked up to a breast pump. The natural forms of inducement were performed over twenty-four hours on average, and they were not guaranteed to work. The second option was to transfer into traditional medical care, which meant leaving the birthing center, finding a doctor, and laboring in a traditional hospital setting.

I had limited time to make a decision. The closer I got to forty-two weeks' gestation, the higher risk I was. And birthing centers don't like high-risk patients because it's more likely they will have to be transferred to a hospital during the labor process.

I was in shock and kind of angry at option two. *I came all this way, did all this work to have a natural labor, and now I was going to have to transfer to a hospital?* The consulting midwife pushed me to choose, but I told her I wasn't in a position to make such a big decision. I asked her to examine me and determine how many centimeters I was dilated; surely, I *had* to be dilated. I'd then take the information, discuss it with Anthony, and make a decision with him. She agreed to that plan and examined me.

After fifteen or so years of being examined by medical professionals, it was strange being examined by someone in summer street clothes and flip-flops! She inserted her green-gloved hand into my vagina and felt around with her fingers. She couldn't feel what she was looking for, so she pushed farther back toward my anus. "Ahhhhhhhh!!" It hurt so badly. Tears rolled out of my eyes, and I inhaled through my nose to cope with the pain. "Oh my God! Oh my God! Oh my God!" I couldn't believe it hurt that much, but it did.

"Your cervix is posterior; the cervical opening is tilted toward your anus." She also told me that she estimated I was one centimeter dilated. "One centimeter! Are you freaking kidding me? I've been contracting for three weeks! How could I only be one centimeter dilated?" I thought that all those Braxton Hicks contractions were opening my body for labor, but apparently they weren't. *Bull!*

I drove home, rolled into the house, and sighed. "We have other concerns presenting themselves now."

We sat at our wooden kitchen table and went through those options, one by one. *Would we wait? Would we naturally induce? Would we trust our midwives, or would we change our ENTIRE plan leading up to this and switch from midwifery to traditional care?* We weighed each option and realized we had some unanswered questions. I looked at the clock on the oven and the green digital numbers read 4:04 p.m.; businesses were winding down their day. We needed to do research in a short amount of time, so we divvied up tasks. I started by asking our doula's opinion of medical groups. Who did she have experience with? Who did she think was philosophically aligned with us? Who did she think we would like? What did she think we should do?

I couldn't fathom switching our *entire* plan, and it was likely too late for me to establish care with a doctor's office, but I tried anyway. Our doula suggested two medical groups. I called one and left a message, hoping for a call the next day. I called the other and was able to speak with the office manager, Alisa. I explained my situation, and she asked me to send in my medical records for review. I was told to expect a call the following day, two days away from the dreaded 41-6. Worst-case scenario: We could show up at an emergency room and receive care, but we didn't want to roll the dice so carelessly.

In my search for answers, I also called my OB/GYN in South Texas. I desperately wanted an expert I trusted to tell me what to do. He advised that I get to a hospital right away. He explained that the longer the baby sat in the uterus, the more the placenta deteriorated and the greater the possibility the baby could choke on meconium. He also noted that I could be experiencing abnormal uterine contractions; since I had been having contractions for weeks and nothing had progressed, my uterus could be weak and might not have the ability to contract forcefully enough. I didn't know that there was so much I didn't know! The meconium, the placenta deterioration, the uterine weakness: I couldn't believe our midwives had never mentioned *any* of this!

I was receiving all new information, and I was flabbergasted that the *entire* plan was up in the air so late in the game. Late that evening, Anthony and I reconvened, and we decided to leave midwifery care and have our baby in a hospital.

I felt stressed and scared, so I called my therapist. She graciously walked me through my fears, one by one. I explained to her that I was terrified of a C-section—to be conscious while my lower body was numb, with someone slicing through my abdomen to pull out a baby, seemed unimaginable. I had never experienced a muscle tear, a broken bone . . . not even a stitch! I had never spent any time as a patient in a hospital, and I certainly did not want to extend my now *surprise* stay by being a C-section patient. I also described how I thought getting a C-section would make me a phony, maybe even a failure. I had eaten well, worked out, gotten chiropractic care, gone to an acupuncturist, done yoga ... all for nothing!?

I was sad that my triumphant moment of natural childbirth was potentially being taken away from me. My moment to shine, my impressive feat, was not going to happen. I was going to be ordinary, and it felt terrible. I felt like I was letting everyone down. She encouraged me to be open-minded, and she got me to where I needed to be emotionally to welcome the baby—*however* she arrived. As long as the baby was healthy, we were all going to be okay. My labor was inevitable, and I needed to be calm or else it could be a real disaster. If I could stay in a space where I was comfortable with the goings-on, I could have a better all-around experience, even with all the last-minute upheaval.

We went to bed worn down to the bone from the day, our pressure-under-fire skillset challenged like never before. But a few short hours after my eyes closed for the night, I woke up with an unknown liquid pooling in the pad in my underwear. It felt like my body had turned on a faucet. I didn't want to startle Anthony, so I tiptoed to the guest bathroom. I flipped on the light to examine the liquid: it was clear and odorless. *Had my water broken?* I wanted to take appropriate action, but not overreact. So I took a deep breath, plunked down on our couch, and started to research. In the darkness of the living room, I read through the ever-faithful Internet, and once I had enough evidence to make a case for my water breaking, I messaged our doula. "Eat a good breakfast, load up your 'go time' bags, and get to a hospital."

I remained calm and wanted to get a few things done before I woke Anthony up, but I guess he felt me buzzing around and woke up. Peeking his head out of our bedroom, he asked, "Is everything okay?"

"I'm pretty sure my water broke."

"Okay, let's go!" He started moving quickly, speaking quickly, and acting quickly.

I told him not to rush and reminded him that we had plenty of time. I wanted us to take our time. It was important to me to remain composed and thoughtful. I showered, blow-dried my hair, and even spritzed on some perfume. He showered and tended to Beau Jackson and Mischa.

We made breakfast, sat at our kitchen table, and enjoyed a few quiet moments. I wanted us to keep our bearings, and we did. Luckily, our hospital bags had been packed since July, so there was no extra packing there! We kissed our beloved doggies goodbye, their tails wagged, and we hopped into the car.

But where were we going? We had no doctor! I knew, at the very least, that *one* doctor's office had my medical records, so I routed us to their partner hospital.

When we arrived, we didn't even know where to park. We had never been inside. We had no clue where the labor and delivery building was. *Did we even need to go to labor and delivery? Or did we need to enter through the emergency room?* We guessed, parked, and headed to the labor and delivery floor. We walked in and made a beeline toward the first nurses' station we saw.

"Hi, I need your help. My water broke."

"Ok, who's your doctor?"

"That's the thing ... we are trying to establish care with Austin Woman's OB/GYN."

"So you don't have a doctor?"

"No."

We didn't have a doctor! We were showing up with no plan or doctor to reference. We stood there and explained that we had been under midwifery care, that they advised us to switch, that all this was thrown upon us in the last few days, and that Alisa, the office manager at Austin Woman's (AW) OB/GYN, had my medical records and was going to call me for an appointment later that day. It all sounded like too much, but we ended up making some headway. The nurses were so compassionate. We were in a hospital room by 6:00 a.m.

The nurses tested the fluids dripping from my body and determined that my water had *not* broken. I had just peed myself! I was *not* in an emergency situation, but I *was* forty-one weeks and four days, and that merited establishing a plan of action. We met nurse after nurse and told each of them the same exact story. I was happy to tell a hundred people if it meant everyone was going to do their best to give us good care.

We were blown away by the professionalism and kindness of all involved. I thought we were going to feel like we had been thrown into a tornado to fend for ourselves, but it was nothing like that. We did not have a doctor. We had not preregistered. We were not prepared in any way to labor at the hospital, and yet everyone welcomed us.

And because God is good, there happened to be a doctor in the hospital from the medical group with which I wanted to establish care. I waited for the doctor from AW OB/GYN to get out of surgery so she could meet with us, and I could beg her to accept responsibility for my care—a *really* big ask. She didn't know me from Adam. She didn't know if I was healthy or not. She didn't know what kind of pregnancy I had been through. Accepting care was kind of like Russian roulette. What if we were crazy? What if something went terribly wrong, and we sued her? I wanted to calm all those potential fears, so when Dr. Garza pushed open the door to our hospital room, I spoke calmly and kindly. I explained our situation and told her how much I appreciated her visiting us. She was warm and receptive, and my hopes were high. She started speaking, and I interrupted her. "Does this mean we're officially establishing care with you?"

"Yes."

We were in business! I was so relieved to have a doctor on board. She instructed us to rest and return to the hospital at 7:00 p.m. Upon returning, we would be checked into a room, and induction would begin.

We were going to have a baby! And even though we were exhausted from the emotionally charged string of events, we had a little pep in our step.

Back at 7 P.M.

When we returned, we stood a little taller because we were there on doctor's orders. The staff checked us in and pointed us to the waiting area. "We're swamped tonight. Something is going on; we're busting at the seams here! Nurses are working doubles, and they're being called in on their days off!"

"Wow! Okay, well, we'll be waiting right over here when the commotion settles down."

We waited and waited and waited. However, the commotion never died down, and we were turned away. A nurse let us know that every labor and delivery room was occupied. She said they were spilling over capacity—one patient was laboring at her doctor's office, and another was laboring in triage! She continued, saying that the situation could change if some of the laboring women progressed faster. Our doctor would keep us updated.

It was my first experience as a hospital patient, and the scenario was new to me. *Run out of space? The number of rooms was finite?* Yet another turn, in our unorthodox road to parenting. I inhaled, filled my lungs with air, and put my shoulders back. We drove to the hotel where my folks were staying.

Because we were so late into the pregnancy—now forty-one weeks and five days—the amount of amniotic fluid available for the baby was a concern. And because they had no space for us at the inn, Dr. Garza sent us to get another biophysical profile. The exam showed that there was a safe level of amniotic fluid, and the baby was in prime position. And, for the first time, we were able to make out the shape of her sweet face and rounded cheeks. It was remarkable. After a complete change in plan, finding the right hospital and the right doctor, being admitted and then being turned away, soon-to-be-rosy cheeks were a wonderful thing to see.

Dr. Garza's Office

Dr. Garza told us to plan on being admitted Thursday night, August 21, and to arrive at the hospital at 7:00 p.m.

"How likely is it that we don't get into a hospital room?"

"There is a slight possibility that we will. I'll try my best to get you in."

At 7:00 p.m., we headed *back* to the hospital for the third time, two days in a row. Frequent flyers. We said hello at the same nurses' station, checked in at the same desk, and sat in the same teal-colored waiting room.

I tried not to get my hopes up. I was forty-one weeks and five days, but until I was forty-one weeks and six days, they really didn't *have* to give me a room. Anthony and I waited with low expectations, and then a nurse turned the corner into the waiting room.

"Hernandez?"

"Yes, ma'am."

"Your room will be ready shortly; we're just cleaning it up."

Just Between Us

Just between us, I fully expected to over perform and for the baby to arrive early. How awesome is that? My hubris knew no bounds. I experienced Braxton Hicks contractions every day for at least three weeks. I ate all the suggested foods, did all the suggested workouts, and stretched in all the suggested ways. The baby *had* to arrive early! Only, she didn't, because ... she didn't! I had so little control over the timing of events, and for a very pregnant, very Type A person, it tested my patience like nothing had before. When I hit week thirty-eight, I thought my body had reached its limit, but it hadn't gotten close.

When our midwives suggested transferring care, I was frustrated and angry, mostly at myself, for having chosen a birthing center where the staff was less exact than I liked. At the end of my pregnancy, I wanted what I had come to expect: doctors, technology, and clear answers.

The change in medical care presented a bevy of logistics that had to be addressed. No part of the plan I had worked on for months mattered. My emotions were heightened, and I felt like I was getting pummeled by waves, but by the grace of God, I knew I needed to keep it together and help my baby arrive safely. God gave me enough grace to stay collected, and I constantly reminded myself that all I was expected to do was make ONE good decision at a time.

Just between us, I am ashamed that I was so arrogant. What a piece of work. Let it be shouted from the rooftops ... HOW YOUR BABY ARRIVES MATTERS NOT! All that matters is that mama and baby are comfortable and safe. C-section, water birth, birthing center, epidural, squatting in a jungle ... they are all HOLY and MIRACULOUS! I'm not sure how or why I created a heroic image of labor. I mean, it's not like I had ever experienced labor before, as a participant or even as a spectator! I allowed my ego to run rampant, and the result could have been disastrous. As one of my labor nurses told me after my daughter was born, "Every baby has their own way of arriving. It's best that the laboring mom set her expectations aside, and just go with the flow."

I constantly reminded myself that all I was expected to do was make ONE good decision at a time.

Hope for Navigating—Waves

The deeper you get into the water, the less you feel the impact of the waves

Sometime ago, I listened to a podcast by author/pastor and avid surfer, Rob Bell, in which he recounted a story where he went to a specific breakpoint, seeking to ride a certain wave. He explained how the first wave hammered him and how he managed to get a small sip of air before he saw the next wave, the size of a house, about to come down on his head. He described how he kept trying to swim deeper to avoid the impact of the waves and how, all the while, his brain was conjuring "what if" scenarios. "What if the waves keep coming? What if the surfboard attached to my ankle spears me? What if . . .? What if . . .? What if . . .?"

Bell encouraged his listeners to remind themselves—in times of seemingly insurmountable stress and obstacles—*It's only a wave*. It's only a *moment* in time; all of time will not feel as threatening or menacing. This pressure, this stress, this situation is temporary.

It's in the moments where panic would be understandable that it is not recommended. In those moments when the waves seem to be crashing on your head and taking you under, *those* are the moments where you need to take the *best* care of yourself. So often we forsake our own self-care because we think it's a waste of time, or it's unimportant. But we are integrated beings. Lack of sleep does not only mean we will drink more coffee; it has a pervasive effect on our entire body system. A short circuit in our mind will manifest as a short circuit in our hearts and in our behaviors.

When the boss piles on more projects than you think you can handle, or maybe sweet, dear mother-in-law is breathing down your neck about how to raise your children, or maybe your children are bringing more homework home in one week than all of your youth combined, remember ...

Wave.

Wave.

Wave.

Even if you're pregnant and trying to prepare for a tiny life to come into the world, it is still a wave.

Most of us would rather life's days be tranquil, but sometimes we look up, and out of nowhere, waves are about the crash onto our heads. If we allow ourselves to sit and think of all we have yet to accomplish, or of all that could go wrong, we might give up. But in those moments, we can remind ourselves that we are worth caring for. And when we care for ourselves, we are able to make better decisions for ourselves and for those around us. Time will move forward as it always does, and with every moment, our situations will unfold and calm will begin to enter the picture.

Amen

When we care for ourselves, we are able to make better decisions for ourselves and for those around us.

When we are overwhelmed with all the details of preparation and walking out our plan, or when our inbox is filling up, or when calls are coming in, or when lists are being made, AND the school is calling because the kiddos forgot their lunch, let's purposefully stop and center ourselves before we allow life's waves to send us into a place of stress and anxiety. Let's have the mental fortitude to remind ourselves that they are only waves, and in no time, we'll be floating in a calm ocean.

"Remain calm in every situation because peace equals power."
—Joyce Meyer

Trail Journal

When was the last time you felt like waves were pummeling you?

How did you cope with it?

What are some ways you can practice remaining calm when life's waves come crashing down?

Chapter 18

LABOR

"Hello, I'm Stephanie. I will be your nurse, and in a few minutes, we will begin the induction process."

I had seen Stephanie the morning before, at 5:00 a.m., on our first go-round. "Have you been here the entire time?"

She told me she had gone home for a bit and returned because of the workload. I was impressed that she had worked a mammoth stretch and was still pleasant and efficient. Stephanie asked me what kind of labor I was hoping for so that she could tailor the experience. I explained that I had come from a birthing center, and I was hoping for the least intrusive labor possible. I didn't want to be hooked up to IVs or receive unnecessary medicine, and I certainly didn't want any pain medication. I wanted to keeping moving—walking, stretching, and using the birthing ball. I wanted to bring the birthing center experience to the hospital room. Stephanie was supportive and enthusiastic, and I appreciated it. But even though I wasn't going to get any medication through an IV, she still had to prep me for emergency access. "Unnecessary, but fine."

After I ate my baked potato dinner, Stephanie returned with some medicine to help my measly one-centimeter dilation progress. The week had been taxing, but the real work was about to start.

She inserted the tab of medicine, similar to a tampon, and very soon after, the contractions rolled in. They came like waves. They would build momentum, come ashore (so to speak), crest, and roll back out. It was late in the evening, and I was finishing off a pint of Blue Bell Homemade Vanilla ice cream when the pain of the contractions elevated so much that I was too uncomfortable to eat. Which means I was extremely uncomfortable, because I *love* ice cream. The pain was localized in my uterus, but then it started to spread to my lower back and even portions of my legs. I squirmed and grabbed the railings on the hospital bed to get through the pain. I inhaled deeply and slowly to try to minimize it.

I was in labor.

Stephanie checked on me around two in the morning. "Pain level four." Then she offered me a magic drug. She explained that it was fast acting and would not affect the baby. She also reasoned that I had a long day ahead of me and needed all the sleep I could get. "Ok, let's do it." She used the emergency portal (that didn't take long) to drip the drug into my system, and in two or three seconds, I was unable to gain control of my body. I was drugged and loopy, and it felt glorious!

In less than thirty seconds, I was asleep and feeling no pain. I relished the two-hour nap and woke up needing to go to the bathroom. But while I was in there, the tab fell out. "Uh oh. The tab can only be given once and the dose is supposed to last twelve hours."

Before determining a new plan, Stephanie examined me, and I braced myself. Her gloved hand went ALL the way into my body. She reached in and around my insides. "Oh God, oh God, oh God—please stop!"

"You're five centimeters dilated but still a -3 posterior."

"That's great news! Right?"

Stephanie consulted with Dr. Garza, and since my body had responded well, they allowed me to continue laboring without any more medication. I was proud of my body for making such good progress, and I was excited that I wasn't going to need any more synthetic hormones. Maybe I would be a hero after all!

hahahahahaha

After a new plan was established, Stephanie offered me the magic knock-out drug again. "Give it here." I wanted to be conscious of what I allowed to be put into my body, and I wanted to be brave, but I didn't want to look a gift horse in the mouth! She dripped the magic potion into my IV, and I slept for another couple hours. When I woke up at seven in the morning, I was in hard labor.

I called my doula, and she arrived with her game face on. She was lighthearted yet stern, casual yet focused, in jeans and yet the ultimate professional. She coached, and I obeyed. She was our advocate, and we relied on her to steer the experience. While she focused on the labor process, Anthony focused on my safety and comfort.

The morning contractions were at a level five out of ten. They were tough, but they were quick. They'd roll up, last for ten to fifteen seconds, and dissipate. Manageable.

When I awoke at seven, I got out of the hospital bed and didn't lie back down. The more active I was, the more I could manage the pain. I walked around the hospital room, squatted on a yoga ball, squatted over the bed, and stretched. I was determined to find a position that minimized the pain.

By ten o'clock that morning, moving around was not enough; I needed another distraction, so we fired up some music. I swayed in my grey hospital gown to Marvin Gaye. And Motown tunes worked like a charm ... until they didn't. At noon, the contractions were at a level six, and I needed more than music to get me through. I needed motivation from outside myself.

In May of 2014, then Admiral William McRaven had given the commencement speech for the University of Texas. The topic was life lessons he'd learned as a Navy SEAL, lessons about attitude, work ethic, determination, and making a difference. I asked Anthony to pull out his laptop, find the speech, and read it to me.

"How about you listen to it on YouTube?"

"Even better."

> Over a few weeks of difficult training, my SEAL class, which started with one hundred fifty men, was down to just forty-two. There were now six boat crews of seven men each.
>
> I was in the boat with the tall guys, but the best boat crew we had was made up of the little guys. Somehow these little guys, from every corner of the nation and the world, always had the last laugh—swimming faster than everyone and reaching the shore long before the rest of us.
>
> SEAL training was a great equalizer. Nothing mattered but your will to succeed. Not your color, not your ethnic background, not your education, and not your social status.
>
> If you want to change the world, measure people by the size of their heart, not the size of their flippers.
>
> In SEAL training, there is a bell. A brass bell that hangs in the center of the compound for all the students to see. All you have to do to quit is ring the bell. Ring the bell, and you no longer have to wake up at five o'clock. Ring the bell, and you no longer have to do the freezing cold swims. Ring the bell, and you no longer have to do the runs, the obstacle course, the PT—and you no longer have to endure the hardships of training. Just ring the bell.

If you want to change the world, don't ever, ever ring the bell.

To the graduating class of 2014, you are moments away from graduating. Moments away from beginning your journey through life. Moments away from starting to change the world—for the better.

It will not be easy.

But start each day with a task completed. Find someone to help you through life. Respect everyone. Know that life is not fair and that you will fail often, but if you take some risks, step up when the times are toughest, face down the bullies, lift up the downtrodden and never, ever give up—if you do these things, then the next generation and the generations that follow will live in a world far better than the one we have today. And what started here will indeed have changed the world, for the better.[17]

So there I was, hunched over the hospital bed, swaying from side to side, my legs supporting my one-hundred-seventy-pound pregnant body. The computer rested on the hospital bed, and I was eye level with it. I moaned deeply and sounded like an African tribal horn. When a contraction started, I'd close my eyes, lower my forehead to the bed, and squat deeply. During the contraction, I breathed deeply and slowly, convincing myself that the pain would soon fade away and that I could handle it. "Don't ring the bell. Don't ring the bell!"

"Again. Play the video again."

"Again."

"Again."

I wasn't a Navy SEAL, but I was pushing a baby out of my body, and Admiral McRaven's nineteen-minute speech inspired me to keep going.

It inspired me to reach beyond myself. It inspired me to be the absolute best I could be. It was the perfect motivation for me … until it wasn't. After a few hours, the video was not enough. And just around that time, our first nurse, Stephanie, went home, and a new nurse, Hilary, took over.

All day, it had been all hands on deck; there had been no respite, and I was beginning to fade. To help my energy, Anthony and Summer held cups of iced-down Fruit Punch Gatorade to my mouth, and I sipped it out of a straw between contractions. But after hours of intense contracting, Gatorade was insufficient. I needed food, so I snuck it. I had run a full marathon before, and I knew how my body reacted to long endurance tests. I knew it would be both a mental and physical boost if I could just have a protein bar or some crackers. So, when the nurse stepped out of the room, I downed some sustenance. I was doing the hardest physical work of my life, so I ate.

As the hours passed, my groans and moans became guttural. I became primitive. I closed my eyes and grunted through the contractions for minutes at a time. The more difficult the contraction, the louder and deeper my voice. Every bit of energy I had was dedicated to surviving. Squatting, moaning, breathing. Squatting, moaning, breathing. Hilary noted how brave and strong I was, and it felt good to hear. My baby was on her way. My body was opening up. All that was needing to happen was happening.

At four in the afternoon, Dr. Garza came in, scrubbed her hands, gloved them, and went in.

For her to examine me, I had to lie down—something I hadn't done since seven that morning—and I was dreading it. With everyone's help, I crawled onto the white bed, and the pain mounted. The doctor felt around my insides, and my swollen hands clenched onto the plastic bed railings. I was still -3 on the posterior scale, but I had dilated eight centimeters. Close, but no cigar. The doctor was looking for my cervix to align and for me to dilate ten centimeters. *What would I have done at the birthing center?*

Since I had already labored nineteen hours, Dr. Garza decided to administer Pitocin, a synthetic hormone that would advance labor. The nurses hooked me up to the IV, mobility became burdensome, and Pitocin began seeping into my bloodstream; the contractions came closer together and lasted longer. It felt like I was getting slammed against a concrete wall for sixty to ninety seconds, over and over and over. I fell into a black hole, my entire body trembling as each contraction coursed through my body.

"DON'T RING THE BELL!"

"DON'T RING THE BELL!"

Anthony and Summer were tremendously supportive and responsive. At some points, I asked them to yell with me. At some points, I asked them to stay silent. At some points, I asked them to convince me NOT to ring the bell, not to get pain medications. At six o'clock, Dr. Garza checked me again.

"Same."

Hearing there had been NO change was heart shattering. Two hours of the most intense pain I had ever felt, and NOTHING. She told me to suck it up and labor for one more hour. She thought one more hour would make the difference. *You can do anything for a fucking hour.*

"Okay, okay, okay." *I could. I could do it for an hour.*

I had labored for twenty-one hours. My muscles had been pushed past the point of fatigue. I could hardly hold myself up, but lying down created more pain, so I didn't. I was running out of options. To keep things moving, Summer encouraged me to get in the shower. The hot water against my lower back would relieve some of my back pain, but moving to the shower sounded impossible. Walking fifteen feet and removing my hospital gown seemed insurmountable, but Summer gently pushed the idea until I agreed. And it was quite an undertaking. The team fully undressed me, supported my fifteen-foot walk to the shower, turned on the hot water, and then held me up so that the water hit just right. I hunched over and my swollen legs shuddered while Summer tended to the water and Hilary tended to the IV and monitoring systems. The warm water felt wonderful, but as I looked down, I saw bright red blood dripping down the insides of my legs. *How much blood had I lost? Was I okay?* I was naked and wet and bleeding. I was both the weakest and the strongest I had ever been.

I had been laboring so long that even the doctors had a shift change. Dr. Garza went home and Dr. Reddy, Dr. Garza's associate, took over. The hour Dr. Garza wanted me to labor moved excruciatingly slowly, and finally it was time to be examined again. *There had to have been progress.* In between contractions, I mounted onto the bed, and Dr. Reddy examined me.

"No progress. If you don't start progressing, we're going to have to start thinking about a C-section."

"No way." *No progress?* I had labored for yet another hour, and nothing! My body had stalled.

I felt hopeless and beyond exasperated. Every bit of muscle fiber was drained. I kept telling Anthony and Summer, "I just need a break! If my muscles can just get a break, I can keep going."

They quickly arranged the bed into what looked like a recliner so I could labor in a sitting position and my tired arms and legs could rest. I was in complete agony. Pain level twenty. My body convulsed and contracted more than it rested. There were only five to ten seconds between contractions, and in those seconds, I was so other-worldly tired that I fell asleep, like a narcoleptic. I repeatedly sank into a full dreaming sleep for two to three seconds at a time. I sat on the hospital bed, in and out of all-encompassing pain.

Boom.

Boom.

Boom.

My body experienced volcanic eruptions, deep explosions, one after the other, with no release. And with every contraction, I became more miserable. I was bursting at the seams in pain. Not ONE moment of relief.

When my body had made progress, my spirits had remained high, but with every recent bad report, my heart took a blow, and so did my will to fight. I had done the best that I could. I had labored for twenty-three hours straight, and my fighting spirit was depleted.

At that moment, I thought of my friend, Ana. A few days before we went into the hospital, she made sure to tell me to take the epidural if I wanted it. She said, "There's no prize because you don't take the epidural. Get the baby here safely." And with the pain enveloping my body, I screamed, "THAT'S IT!"

I needed pain medication, and I needed it right then. "NOW! NOW! NOW!" I instantaneously started apologizing to both Anthony and Summer. "I'm so sorry, I'm so sorry—I'm sorry I'm letting you down."

For a few minutes, Summer tried to convince me not to take the pain meds (that's what I had asked her to do from the beginning), but I had no energy to fight anymore. I needed help. I begged for an epidural and begged for the anesthesiologist to come to the room as quickly as humanly possible. "Now. Now. Faster. Faster!" "Okay, okay!"

The contractions continued pounding me, coursing through my entire five-foot-three body. It took every person in the room to get me in the optimal position for the epidural administration. If I made the slightest movement, the doctor might not be able to inject the medication properly. The more I moved, the more pain I was going to be in, and for a longer period. I needed the epidural more than I had ever needed anything, so I focused every morsel of my energy on remaining perfectly still. Hilary helped me hug a pillow, and the doctor slid the long, cold needle into my spine. Almost immediately, the pain subsided, and my shoulders dropped. It was slow, but I could feel a little less pain … a little less pain.

Relief washed over me.

I was exceedingly grateful for the epidural. I continued apologizing for letting everyone down, but I don't think anyone cared. And thanks to modern medicine, after three or four minutes, the pain was gone! The contractions still came, and I could feel pressure, but it was slight—and frankly, pleasant—compared to the twenty-three hours that had preceded. I was a new woman!

I melted into my bed, filled my lungs with air, regained my composure, and came back to consciousness. All of a sudden, I could see around the room and talk to people. *Why had no one told me about this epidural thing sooner?!* And while I rested, the team took five.

Not having every cell in my body in paramount pain was really nice. I was unimaginably thankful for the anesthesiologist's skillful administration of the epidural. I could no longer feel the intensity of the contractions, but I still had muscle control in my legs. It was the best of both worlds.

I had been laboring so long that around seven o'clock that evening, there was a third nursing shift change. Hilary left, and Kat arrived. She introduced herself, and I filled her in on all that had happened. I explained that I did not want a C-section, and she told me she would do everything she could to make sure I had the baby vaginally. To help me reach my goal, she asked the doctor if we could increase the level of

Pitocin, and the doctor agreed. Kat encouraged me to shut my eyes and regain my strength; hours of pushing were still ahead.

The epidural had taken effect and while the increased Pitocin worked, I freshened up. I didn't have a mirror, but I had an inkling that I looked like I had just gone hunting with my bare hands in the Amazon. My parents came into the room to show their support and lift my spirits. I thought it was terrible that my parents had been at the hospital all day without any comforts or rewards. And so when they came in the hospital room to visit, I apologized to them too. I just felt like I had let everybody down.

An hour later, at eight o'clock, Kat noticed the contractions were stronger and closer together, so she called Dr. Reddy. After only an hour of an epidural and increased Pitocin, I was ten centimeters dilated, and I had gone from -3 posterior to zero! Evidently, the epidural allowed everything in my body to relax and adjust. Hearing that I was dilated ten centimeters boosted my confidence. I was going to be able to do it! My body was going to see me through.

Hour 23

I had labored for twenty-three hours, and the medical staff told me I was in prime position to start pushing. Kat said it would take a while to get the rhythm of pushing, and the process would take a few hours, but she would coach me through.

I was grateful that everything had fallen into place. I'd had a whirlwind of a week. I had carried our child inside of me for forty-one weeks and six days, and in moments, I was going to get to meet her.

A few minutes later, Summer and Anthony walked back in.

"She's pushing."

"What? Holy … !"

I listened intently to Kat's instructions and followed them, word for word. My pain level was so low that I felt good enough to joke and even ask for my makeup bag! I thought I'd freshen up for the big debut. I knew there were going to be photos taken, and I thought some powder and a fresh coat of mascara would help. Anthony could not believe his eyes. I was face up, with all my privates exposed, asking for a makeup bag. I had labored twenty-four hours—hard labor for twelve of them. I had bled, sweat, showered, shivered, cried, laughed, moaned, yelled, and groaned from what seemed like the center of the earth … and I wanted mascara.

"Here we gooooo! It's time." Kat put my legs into the stirrups so my shins were parallel to the ceiling, and my legs created a ninety-degree angle. "You feel it coming on? Take a deep breath. Hold it in. Push from your core!"

There was nothing left to the imagination. There was a planet-sized fluorescent light shining directly onto my vagina. My legs were high and wide for all in the room to see. Every pore, every hair, every single piece of my lower region was on display. I was like an art installation, only I was in a hospital room.

Kat coached, I pushed. Kat coached, I pushed. After a few pushes, Kat realized the pushing was going extraordinarily well, and we were going to meet our baby sooner than we had estimated, so she called in Dr. Reddy.

The nurses and doctors were impressed by my strength and my pushing technique. The more they praised, the more I wanted to make them proud.

Dr. Reddy came in and told us we were minutes away. I could see staff spilling into the room. My pain intensified, but it was a different feeling than before the epidural. When the baby started to exit, she felt like a truck running through the middle of my body. There was so much pressure on my insides; it seemed like there was no conceivable way they could stretch even one millimeter more.

Kat poked around and invited Anthony to look at the baby making her way through. *Whoa. We are not in Kansas anymore. My husband is looking at my vagina being pried open by a baby.*

"There's hair! She has hair!"

How nice, but I still have to PUSH her through.

"Here we go, here we go, here we go. Give me one big one, one big one! Here comes her head, here comes her head!"

I felt her skull pushing against my bones.

"Okay, okay, take a deep breath. Take a deep breath. Hold it in and push!"

She shot through like a bullet.

"Oh my gosh, oh my gosh. She's out, she's out!"

Within seconds, the nurses wiped her down and laid her on my chest. I was in disbelief. I had done it. I had given birth to a baby.

Thirty seconds after her birth, a nurse asked if I wanted to feed her. I said "yes," and the nurse took my boob out from my bra, situated the baby's mouth on my nipple, and while the baby and I made eye contact, she began to eat. She latched on, and we stared at each other.

I was in disbelief that she wasn't crying. She had taken her time arriving, and I knew she felt safe. I knew she had arrived on assignment from God—only time would tell what her assignment was.

A tornado of people whirled around. Nurses attended both the baby and me. "Can you feel anything?" they asked. When the baby's shoulders pushed through, my vagina tore, and they needed to stitch me up. So while the baby nursed, they began sewing me up.

"Yes, yes, I can."

They applied more local anesthetic and went back to work. I could see the thread coming up between my legs. It was surreal. My vaginal opening was being sewn, in front of a room of viewers no less. *What an interesting location for my first-ever stitches.* hahahahaha

After everything was tidy and the baby was cleaned up, my parents came in the room to congratulate us. My mom walked into the room and headed straight to me. I was *her* baby. It was touching. My parents hugged and kissed us and "oohed" and "aahed"; I loved that they were able to share in the moment.

The baby had finally gotten enough to eat, so the nurses took her across the room to the incubator, bathed her, and took her footprints. I watched as Anthony held her and rocked her. He was a new papa. The deep love he and I had for each other had manifested into a holy moment. Alexandra had arrived.

Just Between Us

 Having a doula was a blessing. She was our cornerstone. She had read the playbook and had been to the game. None of what happened that day was a surprise to her. And just as we expected, she helped steer our experience.

Before I went into labor, I asked women what contractions felt like, and NO ONE gave me a description of what I experienced. After laboring twelve hours, the pain was agonizing. The doctors and nurses instructed me to relax into the contractions, to not constrict, to imagine my body opening up, and to allow the pain to wash over me. But it was a tall order to relax into the contractions, and because I resisted the contractions, my body remained … well, contracted.

I really love this

We employed a variety of pain management methods to help me get through, but none worked as well as Admiral McRaven's speech. I was no Navy SEAL, but I was in the middle of unyielding pain, and hearing such uplifting, motivational language helped me tap further into my well of strength. His words shifted my experience from something personal to something bigger than myself and my absurd heroic antics.

Just between us, I was motivated to abstain from pain meds partly because I wanted to appear triumphant, but partly because I didn't want our baby medicated. I had heard terrible tales of babies having side effects from pain medications, and even if the chance was slim, I didn't want her to be a statistic.

To be so wrapped up in ego during such a holy experience was senseless, but I absolutely was. I absolutely wanted to be impressive, and I absolutely wanted people to marvel and praise me for it. I thought going without pain medication equaled more praise, and maybe it would have, but maybe that wasn't the time or the place for praise. I've settled on the reality that it was a time and place for marvel and gratitude.

When I waved the flag and asked for the epidural, I felt like I had let everyone down, but in reality, I had only let down my ego. I wanted a heroic labor. I wanted to say that, like my mom, I had bitten down on a towel and that's what got me through. But that wasn't *my* story. My story could never have been my mom's story or anyone else's. It took a carefully crafted series of events to learn the moral of my birth story: humility. God intended for me to know that we are each his children. *Each* of us is chosen. *Each* of us is worth triumph, mercy, and grace.

After the epidural, there was a respite, and I was so delusional that I had asked for my makeup bag. Listen, *no* amount of makeup could have freshened up the twenty-four hours of absolute torture I had just been through. I had literally shed my blood, sweat, and tears; a little rouge would *never* have helped. I was a bloated one hundred seventy pounds and about to push a baby through my vaginal canal. Blush to the rescue? I don't think so.

I had seen other moms have photo shoots in the labor room, and I thought I had to live up to that. If a photo shoot works for you, great, but if it doesn't, don't feel pressure to have one! You do not need a cameraman in the room, or a fresh face of makeup. You are likely doing the most taxing physical work you will ever do; you have permission to just *be.*

Just between us, do whatever you need to bring your baby into the world safely. We are each created uniquely, and the idea that we are on a level playing field is wrong. We have different personalities, different bodies, different birthing situations, and different babies! There is no contest, no medal, and no book of mamas more awesome than others. It took me going through a brutal labor to realize that my body and spirit *were* heroic that day, just as *all* other bodies and spirits are when they bring new life into the world. *Every* mama is remarkable, and *every* birth is holy and miraculous. I think that was God's "just between us" message to me.

God intended for me to know that we are each his children. Each of us is chosen. Each of us is worth triumph, mercy and grace.

Hope for Navigating—Being a Hero

As children, culture introduces us to the idea of the costumed, caped hero who swoops in at just the right time to vanquish the bad guys and save the day. We were taught that a hero does the unthinkable, fixes the unfixable, and saves those caught in the most dangerous of situations. These are the musings of childhood imagination, yet we often carry them into adulthood.

But while culture is focused on creating fantasies with which we all fall in love, it overlooks our every day, every person, quiet heroism.

CNN's Anderson Cooper hosts a series titled "CNN Heroes" that highlights everyday men and women who make a difference. These featured heroes are doctors, mothers, animal lovers, and friends who saw a need and took it upon themselves to fill it. They created nonprofits for single mothers, provided free medical care to the homeless, built homes for orphaned children, and provided fresh water for third-world countries. They were seemingly ordinary folks who reached deep into the well of their being and contributed in extraordinary ways. Joseph Campbell, author of the acclaimed classic, *A Hero with a Thousand Faces*, notes that "A hero is someone who has given his or her life to something bigger than oneself."[18]

During my labor, I wanted to be a hero, the kind I had seen in the movies. I wanted roaring praise for not only a job well done, but really, for outperforming others. "How did she do that?" I wanted them to question. "Remarkable," they would whisper. I wanted my name in the winner's column of laborers.

But winning and losing were not options that day. *Nothing* I could have done or not done would have moved the needle in either direction. I did not end up being the kind of hero I grew up admiring at the cinema, but I did end up being heroic, giving my life to something greater than me—my daughter and our family.

Let's forget the idea of the caped crusader and step into the hero's journey of our own lives. Let's follow the examples of the everyday heroes who saw a need and made a difference. And as Jane Goodall, well-known conservationist and visionary tells us, "You cannot get through a single day without having an impact on the world around you. What you do makes a difference, and you have to decide what kind of difference you want to make."

"I think a hero is any person really intent
on making this a better place for all people."
—Maya Angelou

Trail Journal

Have you ever wanted to impress someone?

If you succeeded in impressing them, was it worth all the effort?

never

Name someone in your life you think is heroic. Why do you consider them heroic?

Chapter 19

LOVING FAMILY

My parents wanted to be present for the birth, and my mom wanted to stay after the baby was born to help us for a few weeks. I didn't want either of those things. And my preferences in the matter caused heaps of stress.

The birthing center was laid out in such a way that there was only one wall in between the labor room and the waiting room. I had trouble picturing my family listening to me wail while flipping through gossip magazines in the heat of August, and I deemed the scenario inappropriate. I also knew that if they were there, I would be distracted, worrying about their comfort level versus focusing on laboring.

In theory, after the baby arrived, I wanted to hone in on *her* needs, not on hosting my mom. I wanted to meet my daughter and get to know her, and I wanted to connect with her before I handed her off to anyone else, including her grandma. Additionally, having someone in my space after such a life-altering experience struck me as strange.

But how exactly was I going to communicate our decision? What would I say? I knew my folks were going to be disappointed, but after gathering my thoughts, I called my mom and broke the bad news.

I told her Anthony and I had taken a class, and the guest speakers cautioned against having family stay over right after the baby was born.

These speakers were a few months removed from having their own newborn, and they said, in hindsight, that their visiting family was more of a stressor than a relief. I also explained to my mom that the birthing center was not like a regular hospital. There was no comfortable waiting room. I was having the baby in a house! I described how the waiting room (foyer) was five feet from where I was going to be laboring. I told her that I'd feel less pressure and be more comfortable if she and my dad met us at our home once we arrived with the baby, *and* that I preferred they stay in a hotel. I told my mom she was welcome in our house after the first week, but that I wanted one week with my daughter before we introduced anyone else into the picture. I spoke quickly, wanting to say all the words needed, yet hoping a few would be missed. I thought if some of the words fell through the cracks, Mom wouldn't be as upset with me.

"Okay, Catia. You're a grown woman. You get to make these decisions. I'll talk to you later."

Click.

Whoa. "I'll talk to you later?" What kind of crap was that? I knew I had hurt her, but I didn't have the emotional capacity to deal with her feelings *and* my hormones, so I just dealt with mine.

It took weeks and a long, drawn-out conversation for my mom to warm to the idea of me again. But she did, and we resumed our usual rhythm. She told me that, as a parent, she'd give her last dollar to help me, in any way I needed. I, of course, broke down in tears and in gratitude. I was grateful she gave me a wide-open space to figure it out.

In the forty-second week of pregnancy, when *everything* got turned on its head, I was too prideful to crawl back and ask for my mom's help, but I hoped she would offer it again.

Well, the day after I delivered Alexandra, my dad said, "Hey, I have a conference close by on Wednesday. Why doesn't your mother stay until then, and I'll pick her up Wednesday?" HALLELUJAH! His words sounded like a concerto to my ears. "Sure, yes. I'd love it!"

Just Between Us

My audacity was pretty outrageous. In my defense, I didn't know what I didn't know. I didn't know that the changes presenting themselves would be unyielding. I didn't know how emotionally drained I would be. I didn't know that labor is, in fact, a Herculean feat that would leave my body compromised. I didn't know how *holy* a moment childbirth would be and that I would *want* to share the joy with those I loved most.

My parents' presence at the birth was poignant. If I had delivered Alexandra and not been able to share the magic of it all with the two people who had loved and supported me the most, I would have felt a pain in my chest. I am thankful for the grace my parents have shown me.

The first forty-eight hours after birth were a mix of pure exhaustion, uneasiness, and confusion. I only had a tiny idea of how to go about taking care of the baby. I knew I needed to feed her, change her diaper, and get her to sleep. I also knew I was in extreme pain. I was bleeding, I was light-headed, and I was sleep-deprived.

I was a new mother.

While in the hospital, I unabashedly asked questions. When do we feed? How often? When can we give her a bottle? Pacifier? Swaddle? Bath or shower? How do I tend to my nether region? Activity level? I even had the nurse explain breastfeeding.

To have done the most difficult work of my life and then be handed a baby was surreal. It was difficult to move, even in the most basic of ways. Getting up from bed to walk around the room, urinating, defecating, standing up long enough to take a shower—it was all trying. But through it all, Mom knew just how to take care of me, because she had been there before. *She* had given *me* life.

Just between us, I needed ALL the help I could get. I needed help from the nurses, doctors, Anthony, and most of all, from my mother. No one knows me like my wonderful mother does. Even in silence, she knows what I need. It took me becoming a mother to fully realize the kind of love my mother feels for me: heart-bursting, life-changing, all-encompassing, unconditional love.

Hope for Navigating—Needing Help

For many of us, asking for help is equivalent to admitting defeat. We would rather keep struggling in silence, sinking deeper in quicksand with every passing day, than admit we can't do something entirely on our own.

The traditional African proverb—it takes a village to raise a child—is as equally true today as it was thousands of years ago, but somehow we have lost touch with its essence. With the advent of social media and with the threat that folks can peek into our lives on a whim, we have turned into a society of thinly veiled facades: "All good over here! Don't need a thing! Look at our portrait perfect family!" But really, we are no different from the generations that have preceded us; we are equally entangled with joy and heartache.

Many women share with me that they find purpose, joy, and meaning in helping others, but they battle accepting help themselves. Refusal of help is nothing more than pride taking a long stroll. If we enthusiastically offer help to others and show up for them, and yet we don't accept the occasional helping hand, are we strong, or are we narcissists?

Refusal of help is nothing more than pride taking a long stroll.

When life is bearing down on us and our instincts are to tidy up the house or go purchase a new dress—when our instinct is to numb—let's do the thing we think we cannot do. Let's call someone we trust and talk to them about it, cry about it, name the issue, and start to look at it. Admitting that we have hit our limit and seeking help from outside ourselves is a profound action that will rocket-launch us deeper into levels of connection with those around us. *yeah. amen*

In *The Mother's Guide to Self-Renewal*, author and internationally recognized life coach and speaker, Renee Peterson Trudeau, spurs women to create their own personal support system. She brings to light how having a support system can have a huge impact on how we experience day-to-day life. Folks with robust support systems are more effective at work and at home, keep resolutions, weather personal and professional challenges more easily, are less likely to feel isolated, and (here's the kicker) have children who become comfortable asking for and receiving help and support from others.

In the moments when we would rather be cemented in our independence than ask for help, let's consider personifying our pride and letting it know that Bob Marley was right—every little thing *is* gonna to be alright. Let's consider *not* sucking it up and pushing through, but allowing love in. Just as we want to impart our love, empathy, and compassion on others, they also want the opportunity to impart those gifts on us.

Needing help is not a sign of weakness; it's a sign of humanity. When we are open to help, we are both courageous enough to recognize our own breaking point and wise enough to welcome others to help carry us through.

**Needing help is not a sign of weakness;
it's a sign of humanity.**

"Accepting help is its own kind of strength."
—Kiera Cass

Trail Journal

Have you ever wanted help but have been afraid to ask?

How do you think people perceive you when you ask for help?

Who are three people in your life you feel comfortable asking for help?

Chapter 20

NEWBORN DAYS

The first few days at home with Alexandra were too much. I survived, but I was a wreck. I was the on-call food source every two hours for forty minutes at a time. And even though nursing was an insane time commitment, I was thankful that she latched and fed well.

As the hours passed, adrenaline left my body, and I began to realize how injured I was. I hallucinated for days, and my dreams were filled with rage. *Was this normal?* I had no idea what was typical and what wasn't, so I thought it was all part of the postpartum process.

A few days after we were discharged from the hospital, Anthony went back to work, and my mom and I set out for Alexandra's first pediatric appointment. As I headed out the door, I caught a glimpse of someone in the hallway mirror. It took me a few seconds to realize who it was. *What had happened to me?* I was more swollen than I had ever been during pregnancy, my body was a loose gathering of organs and bones, my hair was disheveled, and the skin on my face hung heavy with water retention. I was shocked at who I saw in the mirror, but I knew that the longer I stared at myself the worse I would feel, so I kept moving.

We packed a diaper bag and a stroller, buckled Alexandra in her car seat, and hit the road. What should have taken a few minutes took half an hour. Just as my mom parked the car, Alexandra started crying. My best guess was that she was hungry. *What do I do now?* We were late, but she was hungry. It was hot, but she was hungry. I was in pain, learning how to nurse, and my patience was wearing thin, but she was hungry. With the car running, I nursed her in the back seat, and after ten minutes, I pulled her off my chest and put her back in her car seat, which doubled as a carrier but was attached to a base unit. So I started to unlatch the car seat … unlatch the car seat … unlatch the car seat … except that I didn't know how to unlatch the damn car seat from its base! I tried every button I could. Nothing! We were so late that my mom stayed in the parking lot figuring it out, and I slowly walked Alexandra inside. I waddled toward the doctor's office with a three-day-old infant and a jumbo black diaper bag in tow.

I didn't even know where I was going. But then I saw a couple holding a baby. *That way!* I stumbled into the waiting area, juggling the black diaper bag and having no place to put Alexandra while I checked us in. I filled out paperwork, caught my breath, and my mom finally walked in. "I YouTubed it!" she exclaimed. I had a good laugh and was grateful for the help. Had Mom not been there, I'm not sure how I would have managed.

I understood that I needed to take Alexandra in for a checkup, but it all seemed so cruel and unusual. To expect a recovering mother to get dressed, load a car, get to a pediatrician's office, sit in a waiting room, and fill out paperwork, all while handling a three-day-old infant, seemed irrational.

My entire body ached. It hurt to lie down and stand up. It even hurt to bend over and fill the dog bowls with water. It stung when I peed and throbbed when I pooped. I had three stitches around my vaginal opening, so even sitting in the bath caused discomfort. I moved around as slowly as I could. But even though I hurt, I wanted to appear fine.

I was basically homebound, so I thought I would take newborn photos of Alexandra. I had seen some ideas online and thought they looked easy enough to pull off, so I called a florist and created a set in the middle of our living room. My mom set out for the craft store and came back with jeweled headbands, cream-colored tulle, and silk flowers. I crouched over, my breasts hanging like sandbags, and swaddled Alexandra in a few silk scarves I had. She protested as I tweaked her positioning. I climbed ladders and turned lights on and off to get just the right photos. And after giving it my best shot for about an hour, I hung up my camera.

Before the birth, I hardly left the house because of the heat and my fatigue level. And after I had Alexandra, it seemed I was confined to the house more than ever before. I was her primary caretaker and her only food source. I was working hard and giving her everything I had. Taking care of the baby was all-consuming, and my husband's help and encouragement was vital. He knew it was in my best interest—frankly, in everybody's best interest—that I get out of the house and get some fresh air. So even in the first few weeks of her life, from time to time, I would feed Alexandra, hand her off to him, and leave. I made runs to the grocery store or to get a manicure—anywhere that allowed for some alone time and some distraction.

Anthony and I fumbled around, finding our way: how to best bathe her, how to best swaddle her, how to best keep her warm, how to best travel with her. Going into the start of her third week, we had a teeny tiny handle on things. But feeding her around the clock was a hard go. I wanted her to be exclusively breastfed, but I also wanted to have pumped milk so that her papa could help with the feedings. "When can I introduce bottles?" I asked the doctors.

"Not until she turns three weeks."

Man! Her third-week anniversary didn't arrive fast enough. I was feeding her every two hours, and I was exhausted. Then, around week three, just when her papa could jump in and help, a miracle happened! Miraculously, at three weeks old, Alexandra Grace slept through the night, which let me get a good stretch of sleep. But just after she started sleeping through the night, Austin had a torrential downpour. And when I walked into her room the next morning, I realized there was moisture between my toes, and the cherry wood floors were seeping wet. Her room had flooded.

I wanted to freak out. I wanted to be pissed. I wanted to yell at someone. But I knew none of that would do any good. Anthony cleared out her room, hired a water restoration company, and set up the baby's crib in our bedroom. What else could we do but make the best of it?

Just Between Us

The first week of Alexandra's life proved very difficult for me. I was 100 percent on board with every responsibility. I was all in for sleep deprivation, feedings on demand, and the huge learning curve that is tending to a newborn. I learned to swaddle and cuddle her. I rocked her and made sure she was safe and warm. I did everything I believed I was supposed to—but I was just going through the motions.

I knew that I could not stop long enough to feel what wanted to bubble up. I didn't know how to cope with my feelings. I felt sad and a little bit empty, but I knew I could not afford a breakdown. I used all the right language. "Oh, we're overjoyed," or "Oh, we couldn't be happier," but I had a hard time connecting with any joy. Halfway through the week, I asked my mom to stay longer. I legitimately needed her help and care.

By all accounts, I looked ordinary. I looked like a lady who had just given birth. I functioned. I took newborn photos of my child, I had a chiropractic appointment, and I went to the OB/GYN. My husband and I even went out for a one-hour anniversary dinner seven days after she was born. I went about the business of life, but I felt terrible.

There was so much to learn, and even though I wanted *to appear* as I knew how to handle being a mother, I somehow gave myself the grace to take my time learning about the actual baby. I learned how to care for her one day, one task, at a time. While I fed her, I let my mom and my husband help with her laundry, rock her, swaddle her, and even bathe her. I never assumed I was doing a better job than they were. I did not expect to be a masterful caretaker of our child right off the bat.

And, slowly but surely, I added to my list of skills. One day, I learned how to pump milk. The next day, I learned how to assemble and clean the bottles. The following day, I learned how to bathe her. Each day, I learned something new. *beautiful perspective*

Just between us, next time, I will ease into it. I will NOT aim to take a good selfie seven hours after giving birth, nor will I do an amateur photo shoot of the baby. I was in enough pain to be on painkillers, yet I was climbing ladders and arranging Alexandra like a prop; it was so foolish. So much of what I was doing was my way of reaching out for validation and connection. I wanted people to pat me on the back and say, "Six days old! Great job, new mama!" But it wasn't a time for admiration; it was a time for rest. Just between us, having a newborn is tough. The newborn is trying to figure out why it went from a cozy womb to a flat crib. Why someone is putting clothes on it. Why there are strange noises at every turn. New mamas are trying to figure out how to move around after having their bodies pried open, and papas are trying to figure out how to best help hormonal mama and baby.

Next time around, I will be gentle with myself. I will ease into and appreciate the glory of having a new life in our home.

Hope for Navigating—The Beginning of Transformation

so good

The root of the word transformation is *trans*, which means *across* or *through*. And the day we brought Alexandra home from the hospital was the beginning of my walk through. I was walking the terrain between who I was and who I would become, only I didn't quite know it.

Becoming a mother and mothering my child morphed me into the person I had always wanted to be. It changed me layer by layer, right down to the deepest parts of my being. It made me stronger than I had ever been, and yet also more tender.

But none of that could or would have happened without going through the weird, mushy, uncomfortable moments that are inevitable during the newborn days.

On the way home from the hospital, my mind reeled; I had only a basic understanding of how tough it would be and how much effort I was about to exert. Books had prepared me for sleepless nights, pain, and round-the-clock feedings, but nothing prepared me for the uncertainty of caring for a new life. At first, I was literally and figuratively wobbly legged and weak. Questions echoed in my cavernous mind: *Should I do this? Is this okay? Is she okay?*

In real time, I knew changes were happening, but I didn't know to what end, and a sense of panic burrowed in. *What would my life look like? How would I survive? Would I ever be able to go get a damn turkey sandwich from the sub shop unencumbered?* And because nature does nothing in vain, day by day, my legs became sturdier.

I was talking with a friend one summer afternoon, and he was telling me about recently being laid off, a situation that necessitated he and his wife moving in with his parents. He bravely opened his heart and told me how he was disappointed that he wasn't living up to manly expectations; he wished he could snap his fingers and have a good job and a house with a garden and a life that his wife deserved. The words were different, but his discomfort and wanting for resolve felt familiar to my heart: I knew he was walking *through*.

Over cold lemonade, we each removed our protective shells, our social media best, and decided to be authentic. *I'll show you my fears if you show me yours.* We concluded that no matter what our lives look like, we are all in the middle of some sort of transformation. Each of our stories are different, and the timing is different, but the one common thread is that it gets weird and uncomfortable for all of us just the same. And walking out the "through" is what molds us into better husbands, wives, teachers, mentors and friends.

We have all had formative events in our lives. Maybe it was a junior high reckoning, making the university cheer squad, or being appointed to a community service board. Maybe it was the electrifying moment when we held our loved one's hand and saw their spirit leave their body. These moments are cemented in our memories as formative because they forged parts of us for all time. And yet none of those memories would have transformed us if we had read about them, or theorized about them—we had to go *through* them. As desperately as we would have wanted to circumvent the discomfort and perhaps even the pain or torture of "through," it just wasn't possible.

Walking out the "through" is what molds us into better husbands, wives, teachers, mentors and friends.

When we're in the middle of transformation—whatever that transformation may be (new career, new love, new address, new identity)—it might get painful and unnerving and overwhelming. At some point, we will all feel like newborn calves, wobbly legged and unsure. In those moments, let's gently nudge ourselves to reach for someone's hand and ask them to walk *through* with us. Eventually, the *through* will reveal the magic of who we really are.

"The moment a child is born, the mother is also born. She never existed before."
—Osho

DANG!

Trail Journal

Name a transformative period in your life.

Twenties ∨
All of them.
Ha!!

Did you enjoy the transformation, or was it difficult?

What is a transformation you anticipate happening, and how can you prepare your mind now to relax into the process?

Chapter 21

DEPRESSION

Six days after the baby was born, my mom left town, and I felt helpless. I wasn't sure how I was going to manage. It was quite the pendulum swing from the cockiness I had embodied during pregnancy. In my desperation, I asked my husband for help. He cleared his schedule, and we learned about our daughter together.

One night, after I put the baby to sleep, I rested in our worn, living-room reading chair while Anthony rested across the room on our couch, both of us hollowly staring at the television and hoping for some rejuvenation. Unprompted, with a lump in my throat, I said, "I miss the dogs, and I miss you."

My to normal,

I deeply resented that my schedule had changed. I was put off that I could no longer play with the dogs. I was bitter that the rhythm of our marriage was interrupted. I knew I wanted a baby and that she was a blessing beyond measure, but I was unable to feel it. I functioned and fulfilled all my duties, but I was gloomy and angry. *Set it out*

The next afternoon, Anthony and I stood on our back deck, and he asked if I was okay. It was common practice for him to check in on my mental state and mood. I focused on the baby, and he focused on me.

"I'm not okay. I'm sad, emotional, and feel like I'm disconnected from anything familiar." I was in such a foreign mental space. MY life felt like it had been severed. *Where had it all gone? Was this the way it would always be? Was I now only a caretaker?*

Once I said the words out loud, and admitted as much as my brain and heart allowed, I felt better. Not great, just better. But I had more to say. I had darker thoughts and darker feelings that I didn't want to admit to myself or anyone else, so I kept them hidden in a corner of my mind. I had thoughts of the baby being randomly hurt. I never had thoughts of me hurting her, but when walking down a hallway, I would think: *What if her head hit that sharp corner? What if she just falls out of my grasp? What kind of person thinks such morbid thoughts about her newborn?*

Alexandra was less than a month old when Anthony had to take an overnight business trip. My nerves shot through the roof. *Who would help me? What would I do if she freaked out? How could he possibly leave me alone?* Caring for her on my own for the first time was unforgettable. She cried at the top of her lungs, and she spit up milk down my back, but I called a girlfriend and survived.

The day Anthony was on his way back, my brother David called me. He and his wife Gabby were traveling in Europe. They had graciously kept up with the pregnancy and had even sent a quilt for Alexandra's arrival. It was sweet of them to stay so interested from so far away, especially while they were having wonderful adventures of their own. David called, and even though my hands were tied with Alexandra, I answered. "Hey, how are you?"

"Hey, dude, open your front door."

How nice—they sent flowers or another gift! I carried eight-pound Alexandra to the door, opened it, and … there they were! They were back from Europe! *GOD PROVIDES.* Only a few days earlier, I had told Anthony just how much I missed my family. Gabby and David stood outside my front door, and I just couldn't believe it. I was so thankful for God's grace and mercy; I beamed with joy.

They walked into the house and we settled in together. We shared stories and took turns holding the baby. It was so nice having them close and feeling no pressure. In the first few weeks of Alexandra's life, friends had come by to visit the baby, and I always felt on edge, feeling the need to apologize if the baby cried. I was just getting my mama sea legs and didn't know how to handle visitors *and* the baby. But with David and Gabby, I didn't feel like I had to apologize for anything. They were there to visit, and they didn't need tending. Being surrounded by family brought moments of joy, but I was overwhelmingly somber. Functioning, but down in the dumps.

Later that week, more family visited, and as they were ogling over the baby, they asked if my heart was just bursting with love.

"How can someone expect me to love her? I barely even know her."

Just Between Us

I made an earnest effort to combat my plummeting hormones, but it wasn't quite enough. I came at it with placenta encapsulation and therapy, and even though I was consuming nutritious foods, early on I forgot to eat and drink. Anthony would encourage me to go sit outside to soak up some vitamin D, but I'd wave him off and stare at the television instead. In an effort to raise my endorphins, I did some low-impact exercises, but still, the floor fell out from under me.

I felt sloth-like, less joyful, and more consumed with worry and anger than ever before. Every challenge I faced seemed grave. My depressed thoughts were terrible to have, terrible to admit to, and have been horrific to write about. I had heard about postpartum depression, but I wasn't sure if that was what I was feeling or if it was just the blues. Part of my depression was feeling excommunicated from old MY life. The rhythm that I had had with my husband, dogs, family, friends—and even myself—was gone. Vamoose. Poof! Into thin air.

After weeks of wallowing, I needed something to grab onto, so I went to church and let God fill my spirit. I swayed as the red- and white-robed choir lifted me with their voices, and my heavy heart began to lighten. I walked out the old church doors and experienced the sky as brighter and the sun warmer. And when I got home that day, three months postpartum, it occurred to me that I had been depressed.

It took me ninety days to experience it, move through it, and admit to it. Any sooner and I may have denied it. If someone had called me out on it, I probably would have been offended—as if somehow my chemical depression meant that I was "less than." But once I had some time to climb out of it, once my hormones regulated a bit, I could turn back and see clear as day that I was depressed.

Just between us, it was a full two months before the clouds even parted, and another few months before I felt some kind of equilibrium. And it was *still* a few more months after that before I felt healed, whole, and strong.

Hope for Navigating—Depression

Admitting to depression is tough when we're unaware we're depressed, or when we think "this will be over any day now." But according to Postpartum International Support, approximately fifteen percent of women experience significant depression following childbirth, and that's only reported cases. Furthermore, the likelihood of suffering from postpartum depression (PPD) is even higher for women who are dealing with poverty, marital stress, inadequate support caring for the baby, or a personal or family history of anxiety/depression—just to name a few.[19] In hindsight, I was able to identify with some of the symptoms, including feelings of anger, irritability, lack of bonding with the baby, loss of interest, and an overall feeling of mourning.

I had always been an overachiever; consequently, I expected to perform with excellence in every area—not only mom, but super mom; not only wife, but super wife; not only woman, but super woman. And since none of my thoughts were exactly *super,* I dared not admit them to myself or to anybody else. Although there were a few outward signs of depression, the major signs were swirling around in my head, so nobody had proof. With my teeth clenched, I kept appearances under control.

So for the first few months of Alexandra's life, I glossed over it all—my ballooned body, my bad hair days, my identity crisis, and my racing thoughts. And because my social media photos were always cheery, all of my angst remained concealed. I wish I would have known it was okay to talk about it, to ask for help, and most importantly, to extend to *myself* patience and grace. As a proverb of unknown origin states, "Nothing in nature blooms all year long." *Amen. Not even us.*

We've all had days where we think it's the end of days, where we think we could not possibly have it any worse. But then the next day, or maybe even the next week, the gold sun peeks over the green trees and, by the grace of God, we wake up with another miraculous chance to try again. We are given the opportunity to RISE. Today, we should all know we have the strength to rise and to feel *all* our worthiness and *power.* Let's not worry about *appearing* strong; we *are* strong. Rita Ghatourey rightly asserts, "A person who falls and gets back up is much stronger than a person who never fell." *SO GOOD!*

After bringing home a newborn, it's impossible to do a lot, but it's *always* possible to do a little—to invest in ourselves every day. If we're running on fumes, let's practice self-care. Let's go for a walk, have lunch with a friend, read one of our favorite books, or treat ourselves to a coffee date. Let's do something that rejuvenates us and fills our spirits. *Amen* *SO GOOD. SO GOOD.*

We have the strength to rise and feel *all* our worthiness and power. Let's not worry about *appearing* strong, we *are* strong.

Amen

As I can best tell, I only dipped my foot into the postpartum depression waters. Postpartum anxiety, depression, and OCD are real and run on a wide spectrum. If there is any indication we are experiencing depression, we should talk about it with a friend, a family member, and our doctor. Our mental wellbeing is of utmost importance and not something to brush under the rug or assume will be fixed all on its own. Postpartum depression and the like affects our safety and our children's spirits.

> *"Life has a bigger plan for you. Happiness is part of that plan. Health is part of that plan. Stability is part of that plan. Constant struggle is not."*
> *—Kris Carr*

Trail Journal

Have you ever experienced depression?

If you did, did you reach out for help?

What is one way you can work on your mental well-being?

Chapter 22

REDESIGNING LIFE

My life before Alexandra was full and bright, but for the first few months of her life, my life felt dull. Part of the dullness was depression, and part of it was the hard work associated with raising a newborn. I fed her, cuddled her, and bathed her. Fed her, cuddled her, and bathed her. Day after day, inside the same beige walls, I fed her, cuddled her, and bathed her.

With Alexandra's arrival, my life morphed, and my days once filled with freedom and fulfillment were gone. Activities, people, and ideas that I once engaged in were no longer available to me. I had no time or opportunity to connect. Additionally, I had taken a hiatus from work and blogging, so the entirety of my days was dedicated to the baby. I had one function—caretaker—and after a few long months, I needed more. While I nursed Alexandra, my mind would wander, and I'd think of my life *before*—the days when I could spontaneously leave for lunch with a girlfriend or even pack a bag and catch a flight somewhere. *What had happened to the old me?* I felt like I was a buoy floating in the ocean, serving a purpose, but with the world passing me by.

My old life was no longer. I would have to design a new life. *But, what kind of woman did I want to be? How did I want to exist in the world? What did I want my new life to look like, feel like?*

Faith

As the old saying goes, "The journey of a thousand miles begins with a single step," so I stepped toward my faith. I infused my days with God. I prayed, listened to scripture-based sermons, and attended church. I sought out ways to walk more closely with God and discovered a desire to serve, so I applied to be a Sunday school teacher at my church. I had a two-month-old infant, and I knew scheduling wouldn't be easy, but I also knew serving in the children's ministry would help me shape my week and my purpose. Teaching scripture to a group of seven- and eight-year-olds once a week for an hour proved remarkable. And after a few months on the job, I noticed that I stood taller, and my light that had all but gone out began to flicker.

Marriage

I needed to get to a place where Anthony and I connected as husband and wife, not just as caretakers of our baby. *But how?* I heard one time that if you want it, you must first give it. So I doled out more praise, more tenderness, more grace, and more affection. I called or texted midday, wrote sweet notes, and expressed sincere gratitude. I even went in for a few long kisses at six in the evening. And every now and then, I made sure to thank him for working so hard and bringing home the bacon. His efforts provided an environment where I could stay home and raise our daughter. An environment where we were safe and secure. I didn't take it for granted. Even though we had a tiny baby and I wasn't sure which way was up, I made it a priority to tend to my husband's heart, my heart, and our marriage.

With a newborn, time was scarce and precious, so I made an effort to communicate more clearly. I learned how to ask for what I needed right away. "I need help here." "I need you to take charge of caring for the dogs." "I need time to exercise." "I need touch." Touch was crucial and kept us connected, literally and figuratively. Touch came in the form of a hand on a shoulder, holding hands, hugging, or cuddling. Even if we only had ten minutes, I'd say, "I need touch tonight." And after I'd put the baby to sleep, we'd lie on the couch and spoon. There was no expectation except being together, sharing the same air, and syncing up breathing patterns and heartbeats. I didn't casually wish my marriage well; I invested in it. And with our marriage stronger, my light strengthened.

After my relationship with God and my husband were bolstered, I packed up the baby and took a road trip to my hometown. I packed my car top to bottom with gadgets and what seemed like the entire inventory of a baby store. While I was there, I shared meals with family, attended a friend's baby shower, and even had my first public speaking engagement. My girlfriend, a lecturer at a local university, asked me to speak to her students on goal-setting and success. I was elated for the opportunity. But even with the hours of preparation that I put in, I completely rambled. I was still in a haze of depression and still learning the very basics of how to care for the baby. I had no business taking on a speaking opportunity! I was barely learning how to feed her and still have time to shower. How to dress her and dress myself without breaking into a sweat. How to arrange my life around her nap schedule, and how to get her to nap in the first place! Frankly, the speaking opportunity was too much.

That week in my hometown, away from our home in Austin, was taxing and tested my sanity, but it gave me the opportunity to stretch my mama muscles and learn a wee bit more about navigating the world with Alexandra. And with every choice I made to redesign my life, my inner light grew stronger still.

🪷

Even though we had a tiny baby and I wasn't sure which way was up, I made it a priority to tend to my husband's heart, my heart, and our marriage.

Just Between Us

You know how it feels when you're a kid sliding down a huge slide at a water park? There's a tingle in your toes and butterflies in your stomach. You finally get the courage to stop holding up the line and slide down. You're so excited on your way down, and then, PLUNGE! All of a sudden, you're submerged in water. You start kicking around, trying to find your way to the top. You finally breathe in air, and then you realize: *Dang … my cap is gone. My bathing suit floated off. My sunglasses are missing!* You realize you lost some things in the plunge, so you look for the important stuff, but you let the not-so-important stuff go. Some things resurface, and some things are lost forever. Just between us, that's how I felt after I gave birth to Alexandra.

It was plainly obvious that my "good ole days" were a goner. The present days needed to be the new "good ole days." So I imagined a blank slate and went to work prioritizing. *What would bring me fulfillment? What would stimulate me? Whose values lined up with our family values? Who honored our family's approach to life? What extracurricular activities could I find that would make me a better wife, woman, and mother? What was important to me?* I realized there were a finite number of hours in any day, and I wanted to use them wisely.

For me, everything good stems from my relationship with God, so in my redesigning, I put God front and center. My relationship with God allowed me to walk through the world and navigate each day. Some days, my faith quietly rode along with me, and some days, my faith had more of a presence. But I knew that the more I talked to God, the more I trusted him, and the more grateful I was for the smallest of things, the better my days turned out.

With so much going on, I was apprehensive my marriage would get lost in the shuffle. I married my husband because I loved him and wanted to share in joy and life with him. And doing the minimum to keep our relationship afloat seemed like a terrible idea, so I tried doing the maximum instead. I gave him the best I had to offer, and depending on the day, "my best" varied. But when our love synced up as parents *and* as husband and wife—well, I have known no greater joy.

I lost some of my old life in the plunge that is motherhood, but just between us, I found my way to the important stuff, and the rest ... I don't miss one bit.

I knew that the more I talked to God, the more I trusted him, and the more grateful I was for the smallest of things, the better my days turned out.

Hope for Navigating—Entering Into Motherhood

Most women who enter into motherhood ask themselves the same question: who am I now? Most of us have our identities rooted in some combination of work, family, friendships, income, heritage, and even fashion choices! But when you bring home that sweet-smelling, cooing baby, it all gets turned around (at least momentarily).

After I had Alexandra, my life was unrecognizable. I was living in the same house, with the same husband, the same dogs, and the same white dishes from college, but ALL of it seemed somewhat new and unfamiliar. And in the same way a fisherman throws an anchor down onto the seafloor to prevent his boat from drifting too far, I threw down my anchor and pressed into God. In a harried time, I needed something that was going to be dependable, uncompromising even, and God's persistent mercy, love, and grace were just that.

I am deeply connected to Jesus and God and angels and energy. I am not a proponent of religion. I am a proponent of goodness, kindness, mercy, and compassion. When I began to really know God, beyond the ceremonial masses, beyond holidays, and beyond moments of crisis—when I really began to introduce myself to God and hear him—I was transformed from the inside out. I spent time reading and studying the Bible (not necessarily understanding all of it) and praying, but mostly, I embraced living *with* God in the small moments. And over time, my relationship with God strengthened. I started to see more joy and more wonder, and my heartbeat strengthened; I knew I was rooted in something *greater*.

To me, following Jesus means living a life where your heart leads. It means going where love has not yet gone, into the dark places of hurt and humanity. It means living with honor and reverence for those around us. It means practicing gratitude and giving every day the best we have to offer. Following Jesus was the beginning of a lifetime of miracles for me.

Once my life's anchor was in place, I turned to my marriage.

Way back when Anthony was still my boyfriend, we hit a rough patch. He was trying, and I was trying, but somehow we were missing the target with each other. So I sought out *The Five Love Languages* by Gary Chapman. I learned that to be in a good relationship, *both* people have to be responsible for giving 100 percent (not 50-50). Among other things, each person has to bring love to the table in the way that their partner receives love.[20]

We each give love and receive love in five primary ways, and Gary Chapman helps each reader identify how he/she receives love: physical touch, receiving gifts, quality time, acts of service, and words of affirmation. He also gives readers the tools to make sure that both people in each relationship feel loved and appreciated. It was a game changer for us as a couple. Once we each knew how the other received love, we were able to focus our actions. I mean, there's no sense in feeling love for someone and trying our hardest, only to have it not work out because there was a miscommunication, right? Of course we want the love we feel for our partners to come through loud and clear. Love must be nurtured, and the relationship where love lives must be nurtured. So after I had the baby, when I felt blue, spread thin, not myself, confused, and chaotic, I knew I needed bigger helpings of love. Thankfully, because of *The Five Love Languages*, I was able to ask for exactly what I needed. Love is just love. It takes an earnest effort to make it a lifetime.

In the beginning stages of motherhood, everything is strange. Heck, it kind of stays strange; we just eventually learn to live with strange. Settling into our roles as mothers takes time. But as each day passes, we build up our mama muscles, and we get stronger and stronger.

If we feel like we have just taken a plunge, we should identify what is most important to us. What are the tenants that we'd like to build our lives and our family's lives on?

**Love must be nurtured, and the relationship
where love lives must be nurtured.**

The question "*Who am I?*" will never be fully formed. There is who we are today, based on our needs and desires, and there is who we are next year, based on our needs and desires. What a wonderful thing that there is no permanency to that answer. From time to time, let's get still, feel the energy of our lives, and when we're ready, PLUNGE!

*"Happiness is not something ready-made;
it comes from your own actions."*
–Dalai Lama

Trail Journal

Do you look forward to motherhood?

If you're already a mother, what was your experience like?

Was entering into motherhood what you expected?

Chapter 23

BREASTFEEDING

I always knew breastfeeding was going to be time-consuming, but I didn't know just *how* time-consuming. I always knew breastfeeding was going to be difficult, but I didn't know just *how* difficult. And I always knew breastfeeding was going to be bonding, but I didn't know just *how* bonding.

For the first eleven months of my daughter's life, I gave her a gift. I gave her all that my body had to offer, including the milk from my once-perky boobs. I aligned my life so that I could nurse her until she was a year old. My work schedule—and, quite frankly, life schedule—was dictated by when my daughter needed to eat. I nursed her when I could and pumped for her when I couldn't. Even if I was away from her, every four hours I pumped so that my milk supply would sustain her until her August 22 birthday.

When I first began to nurse, it was a whirlwind. I was confused. My body had only ever been form, and now it was function? The shift was strange. Furthermore, the going between form and function was infinitely difficult for me to reconcile.

I wanted to breastfeed—modestly. So I created a comfortable space in Alexandra's nursery where I could whip out my boobs without onlookers.

I breastfed and pumped milk a quarter of the day, and I only did it in her room, in my chair, alone. Nursing wasn't so bad, but pumping was the worst. It made me look and feel like a small farm animal—it was embarrassing.

During the day, while Anthony was at work, I would nurse Alexandra in the living room while watching TV or in our bedroom where there was a ton of natural light, and it always felt a little like a treat. She could get what she needed, and I could be in the land of the living. But at five o'clock, when Anthony would come home, I would scurry back into my secluded safe zone, in part for convenience, but also in part because I didn't want him to see me breastfeed.

I mean, it was a whole production: get the breastfeeding pillow, get a few blankets for the baby, adjust my top, whip out my boob, make sure the baby latches, get a glass of water, and maybe even whip out my other boob. I knew there was no way he would ever find me attractive again if he was privy to what was behind the veil, so I created a line of demarcation: "This is the room where I'm a mom, and those are the rooms where I'm a put-together wife."

But when the baby's nursery flooded, the little spot that I had designated as my pull-your-boobs-out-in-comfort spot was no more. *Where would I breastfeed? Worse—where would I pump?!* My line of demarcation was a goner, and I was forced to nurse and pump in different areas of the house. I even had to pump while Anthony and I shared rooms—the height of my embarrassment. It seemed impossible to ideally fulfill both roles, wife and mama, simultaneously. It was frustrating and confusing.

But, after about five hundred feedings, I got the hang of it. The stigma I placed on breastfeeding dissolved, and it became a source of pride. I was eating and drinking the best that I could so my baby could, in turn, ingest excellent nutrition. I tried, and my efforts seemed to pay off. She was healthy and hardly ever sick. Her growth was off the charts; she was always tall and hearty, and it made me feel great. My milk, my efforts, were helping her grow. It was beyond rewarding!

But then, we hit month ten, and I started to squirm. Nursing her was great, but pumping was the bane of my existence. I just didn't want to do it anymore. I had pumped and pumped and pumped. I was over it. When Alexandra turned eleven months, I emailed a girlfriend for help on how to wean her. I also wanted to learn how to taper my milk supply. I was ready to have MY schedule back and not have to pump, pump, pump! The bright light at the end of the tunnel was so inviting.

Well, the day after my daughter turned eleven months, her papa bathed her, dressed her in heart-printed jammies, and handed her to me to nurse before she went down for the night. I cradled her, just like they taught me at the hospital, and she latched for a few seconds and then sat up. *That's strange.* I switched sides, cradled her, and again she latched for a few seconds and sat up. *Weird.* We repeated the cycle a few times, until she sat up and faced me. Her olive eyes stared at my brown eyes for a few seconds, and I knew. I felt it—she was done. She didn't cry or fuss; she had the sweetest, calmest look on her face. She was saying, "Mama, it's okay. It's been great, I love you, and I'm all done." It was like nothing I had ever felt. I sat with her, tried to memorize her beautiful face, and took a few pictures; I knew it was her last time.

In the weeks before, she had been nursing less and less, but I had *no idea* that she would wean herself. I had no clue. I thought that I was going to have to leave town, that weaning her would be a huge production, but it just wasn't. She took care of it for me. We shared a moment, I warmed a bottle for her, and then she drank every drop and went to sleep.

After she fell asleep, I cried, and my husband consoled me. I *knew* it was the natural progression—I was even preparing for it—but my emotions were nothing like I expected. My time, our time, that intense bond … had lessened a little.

I always knew breastfeeding was going to be bonding, but I didn't know just *how* bonding.

Just Between Us

I had no clue that nursing my child, while beautiful, would take mental fortitude.

The initial challenge was shifting how I viewed my boobs. They had been all mine, a source of pride, a way to seduce my husband, and now they were only used to feed my child? That's exactly right. And it took months—maybe even an entire year of rumbling with my perspective—for me to appreciate them as multi-functional.

My grand effort to keep feeding and pumping away from my husband was an effort to regain a sense of modesty. But instead, I became lonely and bitter. I was locked in a room, alone, feeding and pumping for many hours a day. Solitude did not help my recovery—in fact, it hindered it. I needed connection and was unknowingly depriving myself of it. Furthermore, I thought that by separating church and state, my husband would find it easier to be attracted to me. But just between us, I was the only one who thought I had become unattractive in the first place. The stories we tell ourselves are infinitely important, for they dictate our lives.

Thankfully, after some months of experience, I gained confidence in my abilities, and I became proud of my level of discipline. I didn't ever feel comfortable enough to nurse in public, but I absolutely did not feel the need to hide in a dark corner. I settled into a place where I knew my dedication to nursing and pumping was a valuable contribution to our daughter's health and well-being.

Just after month eleven, when I stopped nursing our baby, I felt different. It was freeing, but it was also a little sad. I'll always be proud of that year (we rounded out with pumping—I guess my pump had the last laugh!), but just because the year came to a close, it didn't mean our bond actually lessened. It didn't mean our daughter actually needed me less, and it didn't mean I still didn't give her *everything* I had to offer. But it did mean that time moved on—she was growing up. And just between us, it meant that my heart broke, just a little.

The stories we tell ourselves are infinitely important, for they dictate our lives.

Hope for Navigating—Breastfeeding

The trek from love to marriage to motherhood had already forked and twisted and turned. "Can you please slow down and give a sister a break?!" "Not quite yet," life called back at me. The daily tumult of trying to navigate between the form and function of my breastfeeding boobs was wearing. Were they sexy? Not to me. Were they functional? All day, every day. Though I had prepared for every technical pitfall of breastfeeding through classes and lactation consultants, I was in over my head, trying to reconcile my new dual identity as wife and mother, as a sensual being and a practical being.

I had read literature on how beneficial breastfeeding is for both baby and mom. For baby, that meant healthier overall with fewer ear infections, a lower occurrence of asthma, and a reduced risk of SIDS and developing chronic conditions later in life. For mama, it meant better healing post-delivery and—praise the good Lord—a killer calorie burn, among *many* other things.[21] Breastfeeding was the way I wanted to go, and it worked for my daughter and for me, but I still wrestled daily with *who I was* while breastfeeding. I was a loving wife, a sexy woman (or was I?), and now a mother to a beautiful baby girl who relied on me for her daily sustenance. Trying to get the puzzle pieces to fit together was maddening. For a while, in my uncertainty, I tried to hide the *function* from Anthony in order to preserve the *form*, but that left me depleted and even more isolated. I had to find a way to embrace both the form and function, beauty and purpose, of the body that had brought me through obstacle courses, long shifts at work, and the incomparable marathon of a twenty-five-hour labor. I wanted to understand that breastfeeding was simply a continuation of the transformation I had already begun, but my mind barricaded my progress. My body was not just form and not just function. It could be both; *for my sanity*, it had to be able to be both.

Over time, and with great persistence (almost an enthusiasm) for reaching the other side, the barricade my mind erected weakened and eventually fell. I learned that my body was lovely in every way—I just had to relearn its beauty through the new lens of a multi-faceted woman. In the words of poet Galway Kinnell, "Sometimes is it necessary to reteach a thing its loveliness."

We are all multi-faceted—daughter, sister, mother, friend, wife, lover. It's not easy to gracefully flow in and out of each role. The trick is to flow with them knowing that your essence goes beyond the hats you wear. Your value lies firmly in the love, kindness, and compassion that you give and allow yourself to receive, not in your ability to be superb at any one thing. *CELEBRATION!*

Transitions are no picnic—they're even laborious at times—but they walk you closer to the truest version of who you are.

Your value lies firmly in the love, kindness, and compassion that you give and allow yourself to receive.

"Any transition serious enough to alter your definition of self will require not just small adjustments in your way of living but a full-on metamorphosis."
—Martha Beck

Trail Journal

Have you ever been exposed to breastfeeding?

Are you comfortable with the notion of breastfeeding?

What is one piece of wisdom you would impart on a new mom going through transitions?

Chapter 24

HOW I LOOKED

At my six-week postpartum checkup, when my doctor gave me the thumbs up for sex, I was both nervous and happy. On one hand, I was nervous to be so exposed. *Maybe I could hide under a blanket?* I had kept active, even working out a time or two, and felt comfortable in clothes, but in NO way did I feel comfortable naked. I barely had enough guts to be in a dark room—alone—with a mirror, let alone in a lit room in front of my husband! On the other hand, the go-ahead meant we could reclaim a piece of our intimacy, and that excited me very much!

I walked into our house after the appointment, and with a big grin on my face, I conveyed the good news. Just as soon as I changed the baby, swaddled her, and nursed her to sleep, we jumped into bed. Basically … lightning speed! We began to kiss and round the bases, and when we got down to business, my eyes shot wide open and straight out of their sockets. *Oww, oww, oww, oww! Don't ruin it, Catia. Keep quiet—just get through it.* But the stinging, the stinging!! *Why did it sting? The doctor said my stitches had healed. Had they sewn my hole SMALLER? What was going on? Grin and bear it.* One second felt like one minute, and one minute felt like one hour. *Who cares about the pain? Just let him finish. Just let him finish. Nope, nope. I can't. I can't!*

"Anthony, we have to stop!"

Ugh. Total failure.

We had waited so long and built up so much emotion around it, and I had ruined it! I turned to my side and started to bawl, tears collecting in the top curve of my ear. "I'm so sorry; it just hurts so badly." Why hadn't my body healed properly? I wanted to have sex with my husband! I wanted to be normal again! *DAMN IT!*

I was dissatisfied with the situation, so I made another appointment with my OB/GYN. My insides and outsides felt different, and I wanted to know why. So a few days after the six-week sex debacle, I walked into her office and assumed the position. I described what was going on while she examined me. She felt around my pelvic floor, my abdominal floor, and my Kegel muscles. Then she stuck her fingers in my vagina and commanded me to squeeze.

"EXCUSE ME?"

"Squeeze. Squeeze."

"What? That's crazy! How could I possibly?"

"Squeeze!" She commanded again, and I did it. She assessed the strength of my Kegel muscles, then handed me a blue hand mirror. "Let's take a look."

I was on another planet! I pointed at things, she pointed at things, and she explained the whats and whys of it all. It was especially unusual yet fabulously insightful. I examined my vulva with my OB/GYN on a weekday, under fluorescent lighting. *Was this real life?* She explained to me that they had not sewn my hole smaller.

"Oh."

It felt smaller because a woman's body doesn't produce as much estrogen in the months following a birth, which causes a decrease in the skin's elasticity. The stinging I felt was because my skin was drier and not as elastic.

"Ooohhhhhhhh."

She prescribed localized estrogen, told me to slather on a lubricant before sex, and wished me well.

After a few weeks of continued healing, Anthony and I gave it another go. Success! I didn't swing from the chandelier or anything, and I could tell my body was not quite back to normal, but it felt good! I reconnected with my husband, and we began a new adventure together: sex after baby.

I was able to manage my insecurities as long as I was shrouded under bedsheets, but I wasn't sure I would ever be proud of (or even comfortable in) my naked body again. To be proud and comfortable in my skin, I had—at a minimum—to be comfortable with *who* I was and *how* I looked. Seeing as how I hadn't *ever* been truly comfortable with how I looked in my thirty-one years of life, this desire seemed farfetched.

Before having a baby, I was a woman and a wife. After having a baby, I was a woman, a wife, and *now* a mama, and I didn't know how to navigate sex in light of all three roles. I wasn't a sex goddess, nor was I a prude, but within me were elements of each. *Does a mama do THAT? Does a sexy wife do THAT? Surely a GOOD mom doesn't do THAT! Does a strong woman allow that?*

I was positive that a switch between roles was needed, and I wanted someone to show me the way and say, "This way worked for me." But I didn't even know *where* to turn. Who is appropriate to approach with, "How did you manage to feel like a strong woman after birth? How did you balance being a great wife and great mama? How did you manage to feel beautiful during the breastfeeding season of your life? How did you manage rocking your baby to sleep and then jumping in the sack?" For a few months, I came up empty-handed, until I found Jessie James Decker.

Jessie James Decker is a country singer who is married to an NFL player. So far, nothing in common, right? She leads a very down-to-earth and transparent social media existence, and since she'd had a daughter six months or so before Alexandra was born, finding her was perfect timing. Her posts showed me what was just around the bend. She posted pictures and quips about marriage, motherhood, and body image. And even though she was younger, and we lived in different worlds, I identified with her. Maybe it was that we had similar body types? Maybe it was that we were both new moms? Maybe it was that she was so relatable? Whatever the case, finding her was a lifesaver. I found someone to glean information from—even if it was just bits and pieces from afar. She was a new mama, a wife, and an attractive woman, and she seemed *proud* of who she was *and* of her body. I liked that she admitted to not having her pre-baby body back, three weeks postpartum. I liked that she wasn't in a rush. I liked that she breastfed her baby and pumped. I liked that she didn't berate herself and that she had fun with it all.

After following her journey, a lightbulb went off in my head. *Oh! I don't have to take everything seriously. I don't have to be rigid. I can go with the flow! I can even enjoy it! I can enjoy my husband. I can be a mama, a sexy wife, and a strong woman at the same time! Switching roles is unnecessary!* The walls I had erected to carefully compartmentalize my life began to crumble.

Body Image

My once-toned, athletic body had turned pillow-soft, my body composition entirely different from its pre-baby form. I had seen the same body for the better part of twenty years, and all of sudden, I was in a new body ... and I was disturbed by it. Restless, I did low-impact exercises at home one month after giving birth. I wanted anything that would boost my endorphins and help me return to my pre-baby body.

Must fit into pre-baby clothes. Must get pre-baby body. Everyone else could take their time, but I wanted to get there as quickly as possible. I worked out, ate well, and even wore girdles. I wanted my husband to think I was attractive. Hell, *I* wanted to think I was attractive.

Slowly, I started accumulating tiny morsels of courage and confidence, and three months postpartum, I found myself in front of my husband—naked. It had been an entire year since I had let ALL of myself be seen. To be naked is not always to be vulnerable, but in that moment, I absolutely was.

I lay there, my body changed from that of a 30-year-old fitness enthusiast to a new mama. Hour after hour, my breasts filled with milk overnight only to be emptied during the day, and when I stood naked, they sagged, stretch-marked and heavy with weight. My stomach was soft like dough, abs nowhere in sight. My legs were powerful but not nearly as toned as they once were, and my privates—battered and scarred, but purposeful—were no longer only for pleasure but also to bring life into the world. I lay there, naked, scared, and vulnerable in my new body, my changed shell.

He had seen me sweat, lose blood, and fiercely fight my way through a twenty-five-hour labor. He had seen me push a baby *out* of my body. *Would he ever feel the same way about being intimate with me? What was he thinking?* I trembled in insecurity. *Was he wondering where his wife had gone? Was he surprised? Was he convincing himself that I was attractive? Did he still want to make love to me the way he did before?* My mind was filled with insecurities and negativity, and by the grace of God, I found a way to shut it off.

I forced myself to pay attention to my husband's words and actions. He told me how beautiful I was, and I believed him. He was kind and tender, and he kissed me without solicitation—I accepted it. He pursued me, valued me, and loved me—I embraced it.

We made love, and the profundity was palpable. I had come out of my depression enough to be in the moment and realize we were no longer just passionate lovers, or husband and wife: we were parents. We had created a *life* together.

Over the next few months, my body healed and took on its new shape. And even though I wasn't always kind to myself, gentle with myself, or compassionate with myself, my husband was all those things to me. He is more than I have ever prayed for, and loving him has been the pleasure of my life. He inspires me to be the best woman, wife, and mama I can be.

Just Between Us

During my pregnancy and postpartum, I was under the tutelage of all things Hollywood media. I felt compelled to be exceptional. I wanted to bounce back and have it all figured out, right away. I wanted my days to flow seamlessly—to be able to breastfeed, have great sex with my husband, and cook a great meal. And I felt crushing pressure, every bit self-imposed, to have a beach-ready body. I didn't care that I had just had a baby, or that my body was recovering not only from making and carrying a baby, but also from birthing a baby. I wanted to look just like famous women do in fashion magazines.

It was my goal to not only look good in my old clothes, but to feel good too. I had set and accomplished goals before, and this was no different—except that, just between us, it was *entirely* different. What was I thinking?!

Eventually, I realized (code for "I learned the hard way") that I was a new person with new circumstances and new responsibilities, so I took drastic action: I canceled magazine subscriptions and stopped watching junk television. I walked away from the media that was making me crazy, concerning body image, and I flushed Hollywood's definition of *attractive* down the toilet. It served NO purpose in my life, and rather quickly, I was the better for it.

Just between us, it took time to get my sexy back, and when it came back, it wasn't in the same way: it was *better* because it was authentic. I walked taller and held my head high, knowing I was a force. Over the course of Alexandra's first year, ease settled into my bones. I emerged after the first year of motherhood stronger, more grounded, and confident in myself—how I looked no longer mattered. Years of trial and error culminated, and I finally realized that authentic confidence and beauty are not end results; rather, they are byproducts of a soul that is peaceful, grateful, and kind.

If a genie were to offer me a Hollywood starlet's pre-baby body today, I'd laugh and walk away. I wouldn't trade even a smidgen of who I am now for anyone else's aesthetics. My entire being—even my post-baby figure—is better for the richness I've experienced.

Years of trial and error culminated, and I finally realized that authentic confidence and beauty are not end results; rather, they are byproducts of a soul that is peaceful, grateful, and kind.

Hope for Navigating—Body Changes and Comparisons

Pastor Rob Bell (God bless him) teaches on the notion of good versus perfect.[22] He teaches that the Hebrew language brings us the word *tov*, a more deeply layered version of the word *good*. Folded into its definition is a dynamic quality; tov takes movement into consideration. Tov is of the earth, tov is seasons, tov is evolving, and tov embraces light and dark. Tov welcomes grit and flaws and celebrates authenticity. Tov knows that life seasons run their course, and it knows that we are in a constant state of creation and forward movement. Tov flows and actively participates.

After introducing us to tov, Bell enlightens us by shedding light on the ideal of perfection brought to us by the Greeks. The definition of τέλειος, better known to us as *perfect,* has a layered definition made up of "being the ultimate, fully realized, without shortcomings, entire."[23] Perfect, in a sense, is static; it cannot be improved upon because it is complete.

In an interview with Cameron Diaz about her book, *The Body Book,* she noted how the anti-aging movement has convinced us that no matter how many candles are on our birthday cake, we should aim to look twenty-five in perpetuity—that women everywhere are repeatedly apologizing for not being able to defy nature.[24] We walk around whispering nonsense to ourselves and each other: "My skin is not taut." "I'm not able to fit into those skinny jeans anymore." "She looks perfect; why can't I?"

At twenty-five, I was peppy, fit, and wrinkle-free, but I was also a shell of the person I am today. In the eight years since turning twenty-five, I have experienced disappointment, triumph, profound joy, marriage, childbirth, more runs to the grocery store, more traffic tickets, more traveling, and more stumbles. I have experienced more excitement and more heartache, and all these experiences have been *tov.* They have shaped me and pushed me to become more compassionate, more humble, and more curious.

If we removed our lenses of perfection and instead used our tov lenses, how might that change our outlook? How different would our days be if we recognized that we are part of something good, gritty, holy, and evolving? How much would our hearts sing if we settled into the notion that perfect is a great word for describing delectable food and awe-inspiring art, but it is almost too small, too narrow of a word, to describe our hearts and spirits and bodies? Perfect *wishes* it could hold all of what we have to offer, but it just can't. So instead, let's honor the expansiveness of our journeys, and let's welcome the notion that we are, that it is all, *good*.

Perfect wishes it could hold all of what we have to offer, but it just can't.

"To be beautiful means to be yourself. You don't need to be accepted by others. You need to accept yourself."
—*Thich Nat Hanh*

Trail Journal

Name the first three words that come to mind when thinking about your body.

What are some body changes you have been through? Could you have had more compassion for yourself?

What is "tov" in your life?

Chapter 25

REDESIGNING LIFE II

One afternoon, Anthony casually mentioned that he was going out of town for work, and I became despondent. I was jealous that Anthony could work in the traditional sense, and I couldn't. Before having a baby, I traveled once a month for work. And after becoming a mama, I wanted to work but was limited to telecommuting and part-time work until I could figure out just how to travel with our baby. But my husband could leave the house when he wanted, and even go to fancy work dinners where table settings had more than one fork. He was mobile, and I was not. He could hang out with his friends, but I was shackled to the house. Yes, I had chosen to take time off of work to raise our baby, but it was more change than I had bargained for. I was at home all day, every day. I was lonely and stir-crazy, and the longer I waited to express myself, the worse I felt.

After having some tense moments surrounding my new schedule (or lack of one), we decided two things. The first was that I needed backup around the house and with the baby. It wouldn't make or break her childhood or my motherhood if I didn't personally change every dirty diaper or do every load of laundry. The second was that I had to change my mindset of captivity to one of freedom. I needed to stop assuming that I was tied to the house at all times, at all hours of the day. I needed to resolve that I could make my own schedule; if I wanted to go to dinner with a friend or go for a run in the park, as husband and wife, we would figure it out. *But wait ... if I had freedom, how would I measure up on the martyrdom scale? If I had help, was I farming out my child? Do good moms do that? Don't good moms lose themselves in their children?*

OH DANG, GIRL!

I was taught that the level at which I sacrificed was equal to the level of love I felt for someone. It was engrained in me that big love equals big sacrifice. Most of the commentary I heard from other moms supported this belief: "I don't even have time to shower!" "There were days when I didn't brush my teeth!" "I haven't left that house in three months!" It seemed like moms were constantly trying to one-up each other's martyrdom levels. "Oh, you have an easy baby; you lucked out! Our two-year-old baby just started sleeping through the night." I didn't hear too many stories of self-preservation or improvement. *What would people think of me if I was a mama AND had freedoms? Silver spoon? Undeserving? Too easy a life?*

The week after Anthony and I had our freedom talk, I was in the car and heard the advertisement for Oprah's "The Life You Want" Tour. In a few weeks' time, the tour would be in Houston. *Maybe this was the kind of thing Anthony was talking about?* I checked online and looked at the schedule: a day and a half. *Doable!* Much longer than a day and a half would have posed a real commitment challenge for me. I was nursing and new to pumping, so there were logistics I wasn't too familiar with working out yet. But I summoned up the courage to mention it to my husband.

"Hey … so … do you think it would be okay if I went to Houston the weekend of the nineteenth?"

"Of course. Book it. We'll have a papa/daughter weekend."

I felt especially supported, not only as a mama, but also as a wife and woman. A weekend with Oprah was just what the postpartum doctor ordered.

I was fumbling around with my roles as mama, wife, and woman, and I had only begun to find my way. I wanted to be an interesting, engaging, and fun wife. But I also wanted to be a valuable, loving, interactive mama *and* a fulfilled woman. I wanted to have my big slice of warm cake and eat it too, and I was determined to find a way. Going away for a weekend of motivational speaking was the start of my efforts, not only to give my family the best I had to offer, but also to pour into myself.

After listening to Oprah and her posse of electrifying speakers, like Rob Bell, Elizabeth Gilbert, and Iyanla VanZandt, I decided to build my "*self*" back up and continue designing the life I wanted. I made it a point to take as good a care of myself as I did of my family. I sought out a full heart.

I decided to not vie for the world's most sacrificial mama. I showered and brushed my teeth every day. If it was nice outside, I would take half an hour to feel the warm sun and the fresh air. I found an amazing dance class and attended regularly. I cuddled with my husband, and while my husband put Alexandra to sleep, I would spend some one-on-one time with Beau, the dog I brought to our marriage. I even went back to work, and when our baby was five months old, she started traveling with me. I blogged, wrote, prayed, and—after much consternation—hired a helper around the house and a babysitter! I didn't always do the dishes, and sometimes, someone else put our baby to sleep. And because of a few amazing ladies who helped care for our child, my husband and I were able to go out on the town and enjoy each other's company regularly. We were able to break the monotony. Furthermore, hiring help for our family allowed me to decompress and be that much more present—and frankly, pleasant—when I was with our baby. Choice by choice, I designed a life that was rich in joy and love.

Just Between Us *yeah!*

I was tense and angry because I thought I had to give up who I was to be a good mama. I figured that being home a lot made me the best mom, but that wasn't true at all. After being home most of the day and denying myself outside interaction (for fear of appearing selfish), there were diminishing returns. What I could contribute dwindled because I had nothing to pull from!

Just between us, staying in my head was a death sentence for my joy. The more I stewed, the worse I felt. I knew that my husband didn't want me tied to the baby or the house, and he didn't want me washing dishes all day. I knew he wanted me to be happy and fulfilled, but … wasn't I supposed to suffer through the newborn stage? I was fumbling between my roles, and I wasn't sure how to get to where I wanted to go, so I fell into the familiar—martyrdom.

Most of the time, we blindly follow in the footsteps of those before us. But just between us, we don't have to hold ourselves to the standards of generations that came before. Instead, we can hold ourselves to the standards that we're comfortable with, that work for us and our families, TODAY. We can design our lives just the way we want them to be.

And while I absolutely think that sacrificial love is powerful and necessary in a marriage, and maybe in other types of love, I no longer think that the level of sacrifice is a sole indicator of how much love there is in a relationship. Love can be exhibited in a multitude of ways. It took time (almost a year) for it to sink into my spirit that I didn't have to sacrifice who I was in order to be a great mama, and once that idea took root, it was freeing. I'd argue that we have to nurture who *we* are to be great mamas. We don't have to prove to anyone how much we neglect ourselves. We don't have to compare trauma lists. We don't have to make our situations out to be sad or desperate or unbelievable. We can be joyful, and we can lead pleasant lives. We can invest in ourselves, our marriages, our passions, and *still* be great role models for our children. If we want to live a life poured out, we first have to pour in.

Take the time to fill your heart, and pay no mind that it may not look like it used to look. Remember, you have been through something extraordinary, and comparing your current self to your pre-baby self is a disservice to *all* the wonderful textures of life that you have experienced in between. Just between us, you'll know your heart is full because it feels like a constant great big bear hug. A full heart will make you a far better wife, mama, and woman. Your full heart is the greatest gift you could give your family. And you, beautiful, deserve a full heart.

**If we want to live a life poured out,
we first have to pour in.**

Hope for Navigating—Living a Life You Love

Many people have the impression that they are meant for more. They walk around with a quiet knowing that they can do more, be more, and give more of their gifts.

In *A Return to Love*, spiritual teacher, best-selling author, and international speaker, Marianne Williamson, writes:

> Our deepest fear is not that we are inadequate. Our deepest fear is that we are powerful beyond measure. It is our light, not our darkness, that most frightens us. We ask ourselves, who am I to be brilliant, gorgeous, talented, fabulous? Actually, who are you *not* to be? You are a child of God. Your playing small does not serve the world. There is nothing enlightened about shrinking so that other people won't feel insecure around you. We are all meant to shine, as children do. We were born to make

manifest the glory of God that is within us. It's not just in some of us; it's in everyone. And as we let our own light shine, we unconsciously give other people permission to do the same. As we are liberated from our own fear, our presence automatically liberates others.[25]

So many times we are afraid to step up and out of the mold we have imposed on ourselves. We value certainty so much that we would rather stay cooped up in the familiar than venture out and feel the fullness of our wingspan.

After I came home from visiting my gal Oprah, I sat down with a pen and loose-leaf paper and began to write the book you're reading now. I knew that if I didn't, my spirit would become muted, and I would grow bitter. I ventured out from the familiarity of my previous career and life rhythm and into the vast unknown. I had been a blogger, but I had *no idea* how to write a book. And even though I was scared, I remained committed and motivated not only to writing the book, but to figuring it out, to seeing just how far my wings would reach.

We value certainty so much that we would rather stay cooped up in the familiar than venture out and feel the fullness of our wingspan.

We can live a life based on what others do and think, or we can live fueled by a sense of joy, connection, and authenticity. We hold the power to cultivate our gifts and contribute to the greater good.

The same God that created the magnificent, miles-deep oceans created you. The same intention used to create the glorious night skies, filled with burning stars, was used to create you. You are here *on purpose* because you have gifts to share with the world. You were created *exactly* as you should be, not one characteristic left out. You are loved, strong, and capable. You are a force. You matter. Your life is a gift. And when you believe you are valuable, you will fly.

We all deserve to live the lives we want TODAY. We need not wait or pay our dues or live someone else's joy before pursuing ours. When we start devoting our lives to seeking fulfillment, to feeling that sense of magic, those around us will benefit. When we dare to step out and fly, it encourages them do the same.

We can try to suppress the longings of our hearts, and we can try to run away from them, but they will find us. They will find us in the quiet moments before we close our eyes at night. They will find us when we're walking down the street. They will lovingly call us back, and invite us *over and over* again to pursue them. Of course, we don't have to respond to these impressions on our hearts, we can go on about our business as usual. But when we *choose* to answer the call, the world will pull the curtains back, and as William H. Murray says, providence will move too, and we'll get to experience life in ALL its glory.

> *Until one is committed, there is hesitancy, the chance to draw back, always ineffectiveness. Concerning all acts of initiative (and creation), there is one elementary truth that ignorance of which kills countless ideas and splendid plans: that the moment one definitely commits oneself, then Providence moves too. All sorts of things occur to help one that would never otherwise have occurred. A whole stream of events issues from the decision, raising in one's favor all manner of unforeseen incidents and meetings and material assistance, which no man could have dreamed would have come his way. Whatever you can do, or dream you can do, begin it. Boldness has genius, power, and magic in it. Begin it now.*[26]
> —William H. Murray, author and mountaineer

Trail Journal

Which of your gifts do you want to share with others?

writing

What activity, person, or place reminds you of the impression on your heart?

What is one thing you can commit to doing that will get you closer to living a life you love?

Chapter 26

"MORE IS CAUGHT THAN TAUGHT"

By the grace of God, even in all my hormonal mess, I knew I wanted to give Alexandra a good foundation. It was important that I didn't pass on any emotional baggage, and I knew in order to do that, I had to work from solid ground. So I worked with my therapist for several months before and after labor. Session by session, we chipped away at my biggest obstacle—insecurity. My efforts, while commendable, did not hold a candle to the seismic shift that happened when I came across an online advertisement.

Dove, a cosmetics company, had gathered moms and daughters and then separated them. Interviewers asked the moms what they did and did not like about their bodies. In a separate room, they asked the daughters the same questions. Astonishingly, each daughter's list paralleled her mother's.

The daughters had taken on their mother's confidences *and* insecurities. It was eye opening to watch each mom realize just how much she had affected her daughter. One mom said, "I like my legs; they're strong for running," and her daughter said, "I like my legs; they're good for running!" Another mom noted that her thighs were too big, and it turned out her daughter had the same feelings about hers. One mom thought her smile kept her skin nice, and her daughter said she loved her face because it was so smiley.

amen

"Self-worth and beauty, it is an echo."[27] *The way my daughter felt about her beauty would be shaped by how I felt about mine? My daughter would take her cues from me.* For a second, time stood still—like it was giving me a chance to catch up.

I felt a deep, resolute, interior shift, and my life changed.

That ad did for me what I had never managed to do for myself. Believe me when I tell you, my earliest memories are of inferiority. Since the age of six, I had walked around feeling fatter, shorter, and darker than women I thought were beautiful. I never felt smart, never felt secure. I always felt like a poor man's version of beautiful.

I warred with low self-esteem. My entire life, my mood, depended on what my bathroom scale read. My entire life, I wanted to be thinner, taller, and have longer hair, and my level of pride was dependent upon how I compared to other women in the room. My entire life, I was WRONG.

Immediately after seeing that video, I began speaking to myself positively, gently, and compassionately. I began appreciating my gifts. I was a child of God, and I started acting like it. I wanted my daughter to feel secure, confident, and valued for ALL of who she was, and I devoted myself to modeling that behavior for her.

I was a child of God, and I started acting like it.

Having the remarkable opportunity to stay home with her and raise her challenges me to assess my contributions to her life. *Is she getting value? Am I present? Am I giving her the best I have to offer? If I'm the person she's spending the most time with, is that good for her? Am I a good example? If I weren't her mama, would I be okay with her spending so much time with me? What habits is she observing and learning? Am I providing a peaceful*

*or chaotic environment? Does she feel safe, or does she feel on the edge? What
kind of neural pathways are my behaviors helping her form?*

That advertisement was a gift from God. It changed the trajectory of my
life and that of my daughter's. It waved a flag early on: "She is watching
you; she is learning from you. You are shaping her life. What you do and
what you say matters."

Just Between Us

The shift that happened when I saw that ad was the beginning of authentic
beauty and confidence for me. It was the beginning of my security, peace,
and comfort.

I no longer hated on myself for having jiggly arms or for not having the
perfectly toned body. I no longer counted calories. And just between us,
I no longer obsessed over women who seemed to have it all together. I
stopped letting my bathroom scale and clothing size dictate my mood. I
stopped berating myself for being clumsy and for not knowing 25-cent
words. And I stopped all of that on a dime because I NEVER want my
daughter to feel inferior. The price I paid to give my daughter confidence
was finding my own.

**The price I paid to give my daughter confidence
was finding my own.**

*"When the student is ready, the teacher will appear. When
the student is truly ready ... the teacher will disappear."*
—Lao Tzu

Hope for Navigating—Our Influence

While I was pregnant with Alexandra, a friend recounted a story she heard about a dog and her pups. While pregnant and close to giving birth, the dog was hit by a car, leaving her two back legs injured. She no longer had full use of all four legs, but luckily, she could still get around by dragging her back legs. Despite her injury, she successfully gave birth to her litter of puppies and was able to feed and protect them as any mama dog would. Yet as the puppies developed, they did not bound around on all four legs like healthy puppies would; curiously, they also drug their back legs around. POWERFUL.

A sweet gentleman, thinking maybe the puppies needed medical attention, took the puppies to the local veterinary office to be examined. Upon examining the puppies, the veterinarian found that they in fact had full use of their legs. The only explanation the doctor could offer was that the puppies were modeling their behavior after their mother. The puppies adopted their mother's handicap, even though she would never want that for them. POWERFUL. POWERFUL

In *The Conscious Parent*, Dr. Shefali Tsabary teaches us that in order to connect with our children, we must first connect with ourselves. Until we understand exactly how we have been operating unconsciously, we tend to resist opening ourselves to an approach to parenting that rests on different ideals than those we may have previously relied on. The mama dog had a true handicap, but how many of us walk around unaware of our own emotional handicaps. And how many of us unconsciously pass them along to our children?

Dr. Tsabary expounds on the notion of consciousness by saying that viewing parenthood as a process of spiritual metamorphosis allows us to create a space where we invite in the lessons of the journey. As parents, if we are aware, if we are conscious, children can awaken us and lead us to the discovery of our true being. Parenting is not only the raising of a child, but the raising of our true selves. beautiful & brilliant

Seeing the Dove ad awakened my consciousness; it helped me connect with my inner self, consequently helping me become a better parent and role model for my daughter. For my daughter to live a life where she knows she is worthy, valued and cherished, I have to dare to believe the same is true for me.

Dr. Tsabary highlights that methods of passive conditioning are ubiquitous, and if we are going to give our children the best we have to offer, we have to be willing to break the chains of unconsciousness and resolve to walk toward awareness. We have to grab onto the thread that connects us all, the notion that we are loveable, and that we are plenty—not only so that we may live better lives, but so that our children live in their magnificent fullness.

> *"Everyone is looking to be told who he or she is—*
> *right and true and wholly acceptable. No need to*
> *tinker or tweak. Exactly right.* Amen
> *—Pastor Gregory Boyle,* Tattoos on the Heart

Trail Journal

Do you believe you are lovable? Why or why not?

After reading this chapter, how do you feel about your influence?

Now that awareness is at your door step, what is one unconscious action you have been taking that you would like to change?

Chapter 27

LOOKOUT POINT

On a sunny, fall afternoon, Alexandra and I were in her room dancing to the *Jungle Book's* "Bare Necessities." As the playful lyrics of the wise teacher, Baloo the bear, swirled around us in a lively cadence, I suddenly felt like young Mowgli—encouraged to look for and appreciate the bare necessities in life.

Buoyed by the surprisingly meaningful lyrics, I finally understood that it was futile to spend my time looking around for things that couldn't be found. I would forget worry and strife, and, most importantly, I would remember that old Mother Nature's recipes would always deliver the bare necessities.

I held her tiny, fair-skinned body against my chest, and we twirled around her pale pink nursery. I felt a swell of emotion, our connection solidified, and then, from one moment to the next, my heart cracked wide open, doubling in size—I fell madly in love with her. It was divine. I exhaled with a sense of contentment as I realized the bare necessities of life, in fact, *did* come to me.

Every day since, my love for her has grown. And sometimes, when I think loving her more is an absolute impossibility, I realize that I do. Her joy, her SELF, and her.great, big, peaceful soul make my spirit come alive in ways I never knew existed. Being her mama inspires me to rise to the occasion that is my life so that she may rise to the occasion that is hers.

With Alexandra's birth, God gave me a two-handed push into the opportunity to be the woman he always intended me to be. Mine was a journey not only in self-realization but in confidence, in worthiness, and in trusting God's timing. From 2012 to 2015, God was pacing me.

Turns out—he knew what he was doing *all* along.

Becoming a mother made me someone else. It changed me from the deepest parts, and, layer by layer, made me simultaneously stronger and more tender than I had ever been. It made me see the world in a more expansive way. I invest in a better world so that I leave a better place for my child. Perhaps procreation is one of the ways evolution helps us get it together because, what I could never seem to do for myself, I do for my daughter without blinking an eye.

**Being her mama inspires me to rise to the
occasion that is my life so that she may rise to
the occasion that is hers.**

Sister, you are not alone in your exploration. If you feel excited, scared, and confused—that's normal. If you feel exasperated, thrilled, and tired—that's normal. And if you feel heartbroken, alive, and hopeful—well, that's normal too. We are each like gems, refracting the light of our journeys differently, but gems nonetheless.

Desmond Tutu says that a person becomes a person through other people. Pin flag by pin flag, reach out for someone's hand and walk in communion; your journey will be all the richer.

Your life will have mystery layered into it, but you have the fortitude to handle its terrain. Know that turn by turn, you are being strengthened from the inside out. And know that once you have a moment to catch your breath and take in the view from your own lookout point, you will feel in your bones that you have *become* a truer version of yourself—and consequently, are more empowered than ever.

As we come to the end of our journey together, I'd like to pray with you:

May you feel safe, secure, and loved for all of who you are. May you have the courage to be honest with yourself and with others. May you realize that your life makes an impact on those around you and has a ripple effect on those you may not be able to see. May you trust God's timing. You will always have the amount of grace you need at the exact time you need it. May you know that joy is waiting for you. May you know God loves you and so do your sisters, and may you know that not only are you enough, you are PLENTY. And, may you have the courage to become.

ACKNOWLEDGMENTS

Guapo, for being more than I have ever prayed for. I am honored to be your wife and to be walking through life with you. You are a miracle, a handsome one!

Alexandra, for making me a mother and ushering me into deeper, more meaningful existence. I love you and I am proud of you. We thank God every day that you chose us.

Luciana, for fighting your way to us and teaching us more about God and love and hope before we even met you. I love you and I am proud of you. We thank God every day that you chose us.

Dad, for being the best writing teacher a daughter could ask for and for teaching me how to always strive for 105. I could not have finished this book without that work ethic.

Mom, for allowing me so much freedom to learn who I was and for being so graceful through the process. I love you and now I realize how much you have always loved me.

David, for showing me that there are *other* ways and for being happy for me when I figure them out. I love you. You have such a giving heart and I am proud to be your sister.

Carlos, for being my true friend and for being my favorite roommate. You are such a good man and I am proud to be your sister.

Scott, for your guidance, support and willingness.

To you the reader, I give you thanks from the bottom of my heart for walking with me. Thank you for letting me into your hearts and allowing me to be so open and raw. Thank you for appreciating the unvarnished me. My prayer is that the good Lord continues to bless us all and that our spirits be open enough to recognize it.

ABOUT THE AUTHOR

Catia has a passion for empowering women, nourishing spirits and spreading hope. She has made it her life's work to inspire women through her authentic, motivational blogs, videos, and her signature Confidence Revolution, where it is her goal to remind folks that they are worthy.

Along with being an author, speaker and TV personality, Catia is a proud wife and mama. Her world transformed when she became and wife and mother, and she now focuses her efforts on teaching others how to make the most of each day, no matter their stage in life's journey.

Both through her writing and during her speaking events, she encourages people to not only be their authentic selves, but to then take their authenticity and flourish. She reminds them that love has always been theirs.

For continued inspiration and hope connect with Catia on Facebook, Instagram and You Tube at *Catia Holm* and at *catiaholm.com*. And don't forget to join the community book club with your fellow sisters at (facebook.com/groups/thecouragetobecome).

Better yet, consider bringing Catia to speak with your book club, school, church or organization (catiaholm.com/speaking).

"I believe folks are WORTHY and DESERVING of the life they seek, and I help them get where they MOST want to go."

NOTES

1. Coehlo, Paulo. *The Alchemist.* New York: Harper Collins, 1994. http://paulocoelhoblog.com
2. "Job Satisfaction: 2015 Edition: A Lot More Jobs—A Little More Satisfaction." The Conference Board. September 2015. https://www.conference-board.org/publications/publicationdetail. cfm?publicationid=3022. Accessed June 15, 2016.
3. "Apache Blessing." https://www.documentsanddesigns.com/verse/ cultural_vows.htm#t3. Accessed June 15, 2016.
4. Dr. Brown, Brené. *The Gifts of Imperfection: Let Go of Who You Think You're Supposed to Be and Embrace Who You Are.* Minnesota: Hazelden Publishing, 2010.
5. Dr. Brown, Brené. *Daring Greatly: How the Courage to Be Vulnerable Transforms the Way We Live, Love, Parent, and Lead.* New York: Penguin Random House, 2012.
6. Dr. Smith, Robin. *Lies at the Altar: The Truth About Great Marriages.* New York: Hachette Books, 2007, 210-211.
7. Jeffers, Susan PhD. *Feel the Fear and Do It Anyway.* New York: Random House Publishing Group, 1987, 22.
8. "How the Subconscious Mind Works: Amazing Facts and Insights." Powerful Money Affirmations. http://powerfulmoneyaffirmations. com/how-the-subconscious-mind-works-amazing-facts-and-insights/. Accessed June 15, 2016.
9. Roizen, Michael F., Oz, Dr. Mehmet. *You: Having a Baby: The Owner's Manual to a Happy and Healthy Pregnancy.* New York: Free Press, 2009.

10. Romaner, Kim Marcille. "Whatever Comes After 'I Am ...'" Will Find You." July 21, 2013. http://www.possibilitiesamplified.com/blog/2013/07/whatever-comes-after-i-am-will-find-you-joel-osteen/. Accessed June 15, 2016.

11. Johnson, Judith. "Do You Know How Powerful Your Thoughts Are?" February 3, 2013. The Huffington Post. http://new.www.huffingtonpost.com/judith-johnson/do-you-know-how-powerful-_b_4705523.html. Accessed June 15, 2016.

12. www.lawofattraction.com

13. Melton, Glennon Doyle. *Carry On, Warrior: The Power of Embracing Your Messy Beautiful Life.* New York: Scribner, 2013.

14. Berman, Dr. Laura. "Low Self-Esteem Can Plague Your Relationships." http://www.everydayhealth.com/sexual-health/dr-laura-berman-low-self-esteem-can-plague-your-relationships.aspx. Accessed June 15, 2016.

15. Emerson, Ralph Waldo. *The Complete Works.* Boston and New York: Houghton, Mifflin, and Company, 1904.

16. www.elisabethelliot.org

17. "University of Texas at Austin 2014 Commencement Address - Admiral William H. McRaven." YouTube. https://www.youtube.com/watch?v=pxBQLFLei70. Accessed June 15, 2016.

18. "About Joseph Campbell." http://www.nq-b8r.org/about-joseph-campbell/. Accessed June 15, 2016.

19. "Post-Traumatic Stress Disorder." http://www.postpartum.net/learn-more/postpartum-post-traumatic-stress-disorder/. Accessed June 15, 2016.

20. Chapman, Gary D. *The Five Love Languages: The Secret to Love that Lasts.* Chicago: Northfield Publishing, 1992.

21. "20 Breastfeeding Benefits for Mom and Baby." FitPregnancy.com. http://www.fitpregnancy.com/baby/breastfeeding/20-breastfeeding-benefits-mom-baby. Accessed June 15, 2016.

22. Bell, Rob. "Good vs. Perfect." The RobCast, episode 66. http://robbell.podbean.com/e/episode-66-good-vs-perfect/. Accessed June 15, 2016.

23. "Teleios." Bill Mounce Greek Dictionary. https://billmounce.com/greek-dictionary/teleios. Accessed June 15, 2016.

24. Diaz, Cameron. *The Body Book: The Law of Hunger, the Science of Strength, and Other Ways to Love Your Amazing Body.* New York, Harper Collins, 2014.

25. Williamson, Marianne. *A Return to Love: Reflections of the Principles of 'A Course in Miracles.'* New York: Harper Collins, 1992.

26. Murray, William Hutchinson. *The Scottish Himalayan Expedition.* London: J.M. Dent & Sons Ltd, 1951.

27. "Dove: Legacy Campaign." Launched September 30, 2014.

28. Tsabary, Dr. Shefali. *The Conscious Parent.* Vancouver, BC. Namaste, 2010.

Made in the USA
Lexington, KY
20 February 2018